Journey to Healing

A Parent's Guide to Overcoming Child Sexual Abuse

by

Rick Morris

Disclaimer

The information contained in this book is intended to serve as a guide for parents dealing with children who have been affected by sexual abuse. While every effort has been made to ensure the accuracy and reliability of the information provided, this book is not a substitute for professional legal or medical advice, diagnosis, or treatment.

Suppose your child is facing legal issues due to their sexual behavior. In that case, consulting with qualified legal professionals is crucial to understanding the specific laws and regulations that may apply in your jurisdiction. Legal consequences can be severe, and only a qualified attorney can provide the advice you need.

Similarly, consult a qualified healthcare provider for diagnosis and treatment if your child is experiencing mental health issues or other medical conditions. A licensed mental health counselor or medical doctor should be consulted for a thorough evaluation and appropriate treatment plan tailored to your child's needs.

By reading this book, you acknowledge that it is not a substitute for professional advice. The author and publisher disclaim any liability arising directly or indirectly from using the information in this book.

Copyright @ 2024 by Rick Morris
All Rights Reserved
First Edition, 2024

No part of this book may be reproduced, stored in a retrieval system, or transmitted in any form or by any means, electronic, mechanical, photocopying, recording, or otherwise, without the prior written permission of the publisher, except in the case of brief quotations embodied in critical articles and reviews.

ISBN: Printed: 979-8-9881856-5-9

Youtube: @Tools4TeensandParents
www.sayhelp.net
www.tools4teens.net

CONTENTS

1	Coming to Grips with Sexual Abuse	1
2	Understanding the Lasting Impact: Long-Term Effects of Child Sexual Abuse	9
3	Why is Sexual Abuse So Hard for Parents?	17
4	The Emotional Journey: Understanding and Healing the Toll of Sexual Abuse	25
5	Understanding Legal Obligations in Cases of Child Sexual Abuse: Reporting, Consequences, and Support	39
6	Identifying and Addressing Signs of Sexual Abuse in Children	47
7	Preventing Child Sexual Abuse: A Comprehensive Guide for Parents and Caregivers	57
8	Preventing Online Child Sexual Exploitation: Strategies, Tools, and Tips to Keep Children Safe	65
9	The Impact of Social-Media on Children's Mental Health	75
10	Taking Care of the Family	85
11	Promoting Resilience and Recovery	97
12	Tips to Strengthen Your Family	105
13	Summarizing a Safe and Structured Home	115
14	A Comprehensive Guide for Protecting and Parenting Sexually Abused Children	127

Appendix

A	Reacting to Sexual Abuse of Children Exploring the Nature of Sexual Abuse	135
B	Additional Resources	139
C	Parenting a Child or Youth Who Has Been Sexually Abused: A Guide for Foster and Adoptive Parents	141

Preface

Journey to Healing: A Parent's Guide to Overcoming Child Sexual Abuse: Spreading Hope and Recovery

A comprehensive guide to understanding the impact of sexual abuse on families and individuals and the essential steps for recovery and finding hope, as highlighted in the book Journey to Healing: A Parent's Guide to Overcoming Child Sexual Abuse.

Understanding the Impact of Sexual Abuse

The impact of child sexual abuse is far-reaching, affecting not only the survivors but also their families and communities. Survivors often experience profound emotional and psychological challenges, leading to despair and a desperate need for hope and direction. The trauma of sexual abuse can manifest in various ways, including anxiety, depression, post-traumatic stress disorder, and challenges in developing healthy relationships. The long-term effects of abuse can be pervasive, impacting all aspects of a survivor's life, including their emotional well-being, self-esteem, and ability to trust others. It is essential to recognize the profound impact of sexual abuse on survivors and their families, highlighting the critical need for healing and support.

This book serves as a valuable resource for survivors, offering guidance and strategies to navigate the complex process of healing and recovery. Through expert advice, exercises, and first-person accounts, the book provides parents of children affected by sexual abuse with practical tools to address the emotional and psychological effects of abuse, improve relationships, and reclaim joy in their lives. The author's personal experience and dedication to supporting families affected by child sexual abuse underscore the significance of healing and recovery, fostering a sense of empathy and understanding for survivors and their unique journeys. The book's empathetic approach aims to empower survivors, instilling a sense of hope and resilience as they navigate the challenging path toward healing.

In addition to the invaluable guidance offered in the book, the National Sexual Assault Online Hotline stands as a pillar of support for survivors, providing essential services to those who have experienced sexual assault. The hotline offers confidential support, resources for healing and recovery, and referrals for long-term support, ensuring that survivors have access to the assistance they need, regardless of the time of day or night. This vital resource serves as a lifeline for survivors, offering a safe space to seek guidance and support as they embark on their healing journey. The combination of dedicated literary resources and accessible support services underscores the commitment to addressing the profound impact of sexual abuse and providing survivors with the necessary tools and assistance to navigate their path toward healing.

The Author's Dedication and Inspiration

The dedication of the author to his family and the countless families affected by sexual abuse underscores the deep commitment to supporting survivors and their loved ones. Throughout the author's more than 38 years of marriage, he and his wife Janice have opened their hearts and home to numerous foster children, demonstrating an unwavering dedication to providing a safe and nurturing environment for those in need. This personal connection to the impact of child sexual abuse has been a driving force behind the creation of "Journey to Healing: A Parent's Guide to Overcoming Child Sexual Abuse," as the author has witnessed firsthand the profound effects of sexual abuse on individuals and families.

The inspiration for the book stems from the author's extensive experience in counseling and supporting families affected by sexual abuse. Through countless interactions with individuals who have experienced the trauma of sexual abuse, the author recognized the urgent need for a comprehensive resource that empowers parents and caregivers to navigate the complex journey of healing and recovery. The commitment of the author's wife, Janice, further amplifies the inspiration behind the book, as her steadfast support enables the author to dedicate long hours to helping children and families affected by child sexual abuse. Their shared dedication and compassion have been pivotal in shaping the vision and purpose of the book, which aims to provide practical guidance and emotional support to those in need.

Essential Steps for Recovery

The book not only acknowledges the profound impact of childhood sexual abuse but also offers a roadmap for healing and growth. One of the essential steps outlined in the book is the cultivation of resiliency, emphasizing the strength and courage that survivors possess. This approach empowers individuals to recognize their inner fortitude and build a positive narrative around their experiences, ultimately fostering a sense of agency and control. Furthermore, by emphasizing safety and healing, the book addresses the specific needs of sexual abuse survivors, acknowledging that everyone's journey is unique and requires personalized attention and care.

Support and Resources for Survivors

The impact of sexual abuse can be overwhelming, and survivors often find themselves in need of support and resources to navigate the healing process. The National Sexual Assault Online Hotline stands as a beacon of hope, offering survivors of sexual assault a safe space to seek confidential support, healing resources, and long-term support referrals, all available around the clock and in both English and Spanish. This vital service provides survivors with the opportunity to talk through their experiences with trained specialists, ensuring that they receive the support and guidance needed to begin their journey to healing and recovery.

In addition to the invaluable support provided by the National Sexual Assault Online Hotline, "The Sexual Healing Journey: A Guide for Survivors of Sexual Abuse" by Wendy Maltz offers an empowering resource for survivors. The book not only provides expert advice and techniques but also incorporates first-person accounts, allowing readers to connect with the real-life experiences of others who have gone through similar challenges. By offering a comprehensive program for healing, the book equips survivors with the tools to identify and eliminate the negative effects of sexual abuse, empowering them to take control of their journey to recovery. With the Online Hotline serving as a lifeline for survivors and "The Sexual Healing Journey" providing a profound source of guidance, survivors are supported on multiple fronts as they navigate the path to healing and restoration.

Spreading Hope and Recovery

As survivors of sexual abuse navigate their healing journey, it's essential for them to not only find solace and recovery for themselves but also to extend a helping hand to others who may be going through similar experiences. "Journey to Healing: A Parent's Guide to Overcoming Child Sexual Abuse" emphasizes the significance of survivors sharing their stories of hope and resilience with others who are on the path to recovery. By creating a community of support and understanding, survivors can empower each other and foster a sense of resilience that is crucial in the healing process. For instance, survivors can share their experiences in support groups, online forums, or by participating in awareness campaigns, ultimately bringing a ray of hope to those who are still struggling to find their way through the aftermath of sexual abuse.

The dedication to spreading hope and recovery is not only limited to the survivors themselves but also extends to those who come in contact with the book. The author's intention is for the readers to not only absorb the valuable insights and guidance provided but also to become advocates for positive change. By sharing the knowledge and support gained from "Journey to Healing: A Parent's Guide to Overcoming Child Sexual Abuse" with friends, family members, and their community, readers can play an active role in breaking the stigma surrounding sexual abuse and promoting a culture of empathy and understanding. The revised edition of "The Sexual Healing Journey" reflects the commitment to providing continuous support and guidance to survivors by incorporating new resources and updated materials, reinforcing the message of hope and recovery. This enables survivors to access a wider range of tools and information that can aid them in their healing process, further strengthening the message of resilience and empowerment.

U.S. National Sexual Assault Hotline (Available 24 hours)
1-800-656-4673

A Word from the Writer

In the holy fabric of life, we are often woven into the lives of others. Each thread carries a story of struggle, strength, and, in the end, healing. As the author of "Journey to Healing: A Parent's Guide to Overcoming Child Sexual Abuse," I begin a deep exploration. I draw from my 38 years of marriage to my wonderful wife Janice and my career of giving children and families hope and direction.

This book is not only a personal journey but a collective odyssey, a testament to the strength and resilience of families who have faced the harrowing impact of child sexual abuse. It is dedicated to my three adult sons and their families, my eight grandchildren, and one great-granddaughter – the heartbeat of my existence. They have been my pillars of support, understanding the sacrifices made for the countless hours spent in the office, striving to mend the broken pieces of shattered innocence.

As a counselor, I have witnessed families enter my office in the depths of despair, seeking solace and direction. This book is an offering, a guide born from the blend of their stories and my experiences. It's a beacon of hope for those who have walked the painful path of intrafamilial sexual abuse, illustrating that healing and safety are not just aspirations but attainable realities.

To the families affected by the darkness of abuse, this work is a tribute to your resilience, a recognition of the courage it takes to confront the shadows and emerge into the light. It is dedicated to those who have found healing and to those still on the journey, with the hope that they will pass on the torch of resilience and hope, becoming beacons for others to find recovery.

May this book be a companion on your journey, a source of guidance and understanding, and a testament to the enduring power of the human spirit to rise above adversity and embrace the path to healing.

| 1 |

Journey to Healing:
A Parent's Guide to Overcoming Child Sexual Abuse

Coming to Grips with Sexual Abuse

It is horrible when an adult or older child forces sexual behavior on a child. This is called child sexual abuse. What's going on is very upsetting and can have bad, long-lasting effects on the child's physical, social, and mental health. When brothers hurt each other physically or sexually, that's called family abuse. We must pay the greatest attention to and stop both types of abuse.

It's shocking how common and harmful child sexual abuse is. The US Centers for Disease Control and Prevention (CDC) says that about 1 in 4 girls and 1 in 13 boys are sexually abused before they turn 18. There are many effects these traumatic events can have, such as anxiety, sadness, post-traumatic stress disorder (PTSD), and trouble making good relationships.

Fighting and stopping child sexual abuse is the most essential thing that can be done to keep children safe and help those who have been abused. We can improve the world for our children by educating people, spreading the word, and taking positive steps.

Journey to Healing:

Recognizing Signs & Symptoms of Child Sexual Abuse

Knowing the symptoms and signs of child sexual abuse is important for finding it early and helping the child. Children who have been sexually abused may show a range of behaviors, such as mood swings, changes in behavior, withdrawal, violence, or acting in a sexualized way. Fear, worry, sadness, low self-esteem, or acting in ways that hurt yourself are all emotional signs. Physical signs can also include accidents that you can't explain, trouble walking or sitting, pain or burning in the genital area, or other physical discomforts.

It is crucial to get help from qualified mental health workers who know how to properly evaluate and spot signs of child sexual abuse. Professionals in this field can give the child and their family the support and direction they need as they heal. For instance, a child who has been sexually abused might suddenly change how they act, like becoming shy and avoiding social situations. They might also show signs of worry, like being more antsy and having trouble focusing. Getting professional help can help you spot these signs and give the child the right kind of support.

Protecting and Supporting Your Sexually Abused Child

Making sure a child who has been sexually mistreated feels safe and cared for is an important part of protecting and helping them. Setting up clear lines of communication is very important. Encourage the child to talk about their feelings and offer a safe, nonjudgmental space to listen. That way, we can help the child feel heard, accepted, and understood.

For the child's physical and mental safety, it is very important to set clear limits and safety steps. This could mean setting rules and directions to keep the child safe from more harm. For example, parents can set rules about who can see their child and keep a close eye on how they connect with other people.

Specialized therapy can also be very helpful for children who have been sexually abused. Therapy services are designed to help these children feel better by giving them support, advice, and healing. These lessons can help the child learn how to deal with stress, become more resilient, and get over the pain and confusion they've been through.

For example, parents of a child who has been sexually abused can make sure their home is a safe place for their child where no harm can happen. Also, closely watching the child's relationships with others can include putting locks on doors and windows and other safety steps. This way, parents can help their children feel safe and secure again.

Parenting Strategies for Healing and Recovery

When you're a parent of a child who has been sexually abused, understanding and support are very important for helping them heal and get better. It's important to understand and accept the child's thoughts and feelings and to stress that they are not responsible for what has happened. These steps will help them feel better about their own worth and boost their self-esteem.

Another important part of being a parent to a child who has been sexually abused is building trust. To rebuild trust with the child, you need to be consistent, dependable, and understanding. Parents should try to be dependable sources of support and make sure their children have a safe place to talk about their feelings and thoughts without worrying about being judged or rejected.

Parents and families who have been sexually abused as children can get help and advice from therapy sessions. These sessions can also help parents deal with the problems they may be facing while also helping their children heal and recover.

For example, parents can listen with empathy when their child talks about their feelings, giving them a safe place to talk about their feelings. This can help parents understand how their child feels and build trust and safety in their relationship with their child.

Addressing Sibling Abuse within the Family

Abuse between siblings can significantly affect how the family works. If you see any of these signs, you should act quickly and effectively to stop the abuse of your siblings. For siblings to talk about and solve problems, they need to be able to talk to each other openly and honestly.

Setting clear limits is important for encouraging healthy, respectful relationships between brothers. Parents should make rules that stress respecting each other and ensure that each child's physical and emotional limits are honored. In this way, parents can make a space that encourages good relationships between siblings.

It can be helpful to get specialized therapy when dealing with sibling abuse becomes hard. These can help siblings get along better with each other by giving them tools and techniques. For example, parents can promote open communication by holding regular family meetings where everyone can share their worries and thoughts. Parents can help solve problems and encourage better relationships between siblings by making a safe place for open communication.

Resources and Support for Families Dealing with Intrafamilial Abuse

Families who are dealing with abuse within the family need to be able to get tools and help to get through the problems they are having. Helplines and groups in your community can give you helpful information about the available tools and help in your area. Support groups can also help families connect with others going through the same problems, making them feel like they fit in and that someone understands them.

Families can talk about their problems in a safe and private setting during these therapy meetings, get help, and work on healing and recovery. For instance, local groups and helplines can tell families about legal resources, emergency housing, and therapy services available in their area. Families can get the help they need to deal with the complicated issues of abuse within the family by using these tools.

Nurturing Healthy Curiosity and Boundaries in Children

As a parent, you must ensure your children have healthy interests and know how to set personal limits. Children can learn to wonder about the world around them and experience it better if you encourage their natural interest at the right age. Making it a safe, supportive place and encouraging healthy discovery and interest is vital.

Also, parents should teach their children how to set personal limits early. Teaching children how important it is to respect their own and others' limits builds understanding and good relationships. For this reason, parents can help their children set healthy limits and behave appropriately around other people. This supports the natural curiosity about their own bodies is natural.

For example, parents can spark their children's interests by giving them books, toys, and activities that are right for their age and let them explore and learn. Parents can help their children love learning and grow intellectually by doing these things.

Understanding Child Abuse Prevention

To stop sexual abuse of children, groups, organizations, and people must work together and act. Campaigns for education and knowledge are very important for teaching people how to spot and report cases of potential child abuse. By making people more aware, we can give them the power to do something to protect children from harm.

Participation from the community is another important part of stopping child abuse. People in the community, like schools, faith groups, and neighborhood groups, need to work together to make the community a safe place for children. We can set up support networks and ensure children's safety in our neighborhoods if we all work together.

Healing and Recovery Process for Sexually Abused Children

For children who have been sexually mistreated, healing and getting better is a process that takes time and steps. I want to help children understand that their mending process is different and that it might take some time for them to feel safe and healthy again.

Therapy meetings, both one-on-one and in groups, are beneficial for healing and getting better. These meetings give children a safe and helpful place to talk about their feelings, learn new ways to deal with problems, and work through the trauma they've been through. Children who go to therapy can better understand what happened to them, become more resilient, and feel more in control of their lives.

For the healing and recovery process, getting help and advice from qualified mental health experts is very important. These professionals are skilled and knowledgeable enough to provide therapy methods for each child and meet their needs.

To sum up, protecting and raising a child who has been sexually abused takes understanding, support, and kindness. Abuse of children and siblings is a significant problem that needs our help and care. We need to stop these kinds of abuse right away to keep children safe and give them the help they need to heal and get better.

A good resource for families dealing with child sexual abuse and sibling abuse is to find a therapy center that is qualified and skilled. Their specialized therapy meetings help people, teens, and families get better by giving them support, direction, and healing. Specialists can make a difference in the lives of children who have been sexually mistreated and their families by getting them help and support. Together, we can make the world a safer and better place for all children.

RESOURCES

- Darkness to Light (d2l.org): Provides resources and training on preventing child sexual abuse, including information for parents on recognizing and responding to signs of abuse.
- Childhelp (childhelp.org): Offers resources and support for parents dealing with child abuse, including a helpline and information on intervention.
- National Children's Alliance (nca-online.org): Focuses on child advocacy and provides resources for parents dealing with child sexual abuse, including information on the legal process.
- Stop It Now! (stopitnow.org): Offers resources for parents to prevent child sexual abuse and guides recognizing and responding to concerning behaviors.
- The National Center for Victims of Crime (victimsofcrime.org): Provides information for parents on understanding and responding to child sexual abuse, including resources on reporting and legal proceedings.
- NSPCC (nspcc.org.uk): The UK-based National Society for the Prevention of Cruelty to Children offers resources and guidance for parents on child protection, including sexual abuse.
- American Academy of Pediatrics (aap.org): Provides articles and guidance on recognizing and preventing child sexual abuse, with a focus on health and well-being.
- Prevent Child Abuse America (preventchildabuse.org): Offers resources for parents aimed at preventing child abuse, including information on recognizing signs of abuse and promoting healthy parenting practices.
- Child Welfare Information Gateway (childwelfare.gov): Provides resources on child abuse prevention, intervention, and recovery for parents, caregivers, and professionals.
- RAINN (rainn.org): Although primarily focused on adult survivors, RAINN offers resources that may be relevant for parents, including guidance on supporting child survivors.

| 2 |

Understanding the Lasting Impact: Long-Term Effects of Child Sexual Abuse

Child sexual abuse is an unfortunate and common problem that affects many children all over the world. Child sexual abuse is when a child is involved in sexual behaviors that they don't fully understand and can't agree to. It is essential to know about the long-term effects of child sexual abuse to raise awareness, offer support, and lessen the long-term effects on the mental and emotional health of survivors.

Child sexual abuse can have terrible long-term effects on the mental, emotional, and physical health of those who have been abused. It is essential to be aware of and deal with these effects so that people can get the right help and support. We can help stop more harm from happening and help people heal by learning about the long-term effects of sexual abuse on children.

Understanding Child Sexual Abuse
Child sexual abuse includes a lot of different actions, such as touching a child inappropriately, using pornography to take advantage of them, training them online, or exposing them to sexual acts. This is a scary fact that affects millions of children around the world. Understanding child sexual abuse is important because it helps you see the different ways it happens and the short- and long-term harm it does to the victims.

As an example, any kind of touching or sexual act done on a child without their permission is considered physical contact abuse. In this group are things like fondling, rape, and forced oral sex. When sexually explicit material with children is made, distributed, or watched, this is called exploitation through pornography. This can hurt the victims for a long time because other people may be able to see and use their image for years to come. When an adult starts a friendship with a child online, usually to sexually abuse them; this is called "online grooming." Eventually, this can lead to child sexual exploitation.

It is essential to know the different types of sexual abuse of children so that you can spot them and help. We can take steps to protect children and stop more harm from happening if we know the signs and actions of child sexual abuse.

Psychological Effects of Child Sexual Abuse

Sexual abuse of children can have very bad and long-lasting effects on their mental health. Some of these are worry, sadness, dissociation, suicidal thoughts, and post-traumatic stress disorder (PTSD). Survivors often have trouble trusting others, low self-esteem, feelings of shame and guilt, and a skewed view of who they are. Abuse can have a big effect on their sense of self-worth, self-esteem, and body image, making them feel useless and giving them a bad view of their bodies.

For instance, someone who has been sexually abused as a child may develop PTSD and have flashbacks, nightmares, and intense fear or anxiety about the painful event. They may also have problems with depression, which makes them sad, helpless, and less interested in things they used to enjoy. Dissociation is a state in which survivors of abuse may not feel linked to their bodies or have trouble remembering parts of the abuse. It can be caused by mental pain and trauma.

Child sexual abuse can have long-lasting effects on a person's mental health that can affect many areas of their life. It is very important to help people heal and feel like they have control over their lives again by giving them the right treatment and support.

Emotional Effects of Child Sexual Abuse

Sexual abuse of children has a huge effect on their mental health. Fear, anger, sadness, shame, and doubt are just some of the feelings that can come up because of it. Survivors may have a hard time controlling their feelings, which can cause big mood swings. They may also have trouble expressing their feelings in a healthy way and develop unhealthy ways to deal with stress. Child sexual abuse can also make it very hard for survivors to make and keep good relationships because it often hurts their trust in others and makes it hard for them to get close to others.

For example, a victim may feel a lot of fear and worry because they don't trust other people and are afraid of getting hurt again. Besides that, they might feel very angry at either the attacker or themselves for not being able to stop it. Shame and guilt are also common. Survivors may wrongly blame themselves for the abuse or feel bad about their bodies and what they went through in the past.

Child sexual abuse can have substantial mental effects that can get in the way of a survivor's daily life and relationships. It is very important to give people a safe and helpful place to talk about and work through their feelings and to help them learn healthy ways to deal with stress.

Long-Term Consequences in Adulthood

Sexual abuse as a child can have long-lasting effects on a person's mind and emotions, even as an adult. Mental health problems like sadness, anxiety disorders, drug abuse, eating disorders, and borderline personality disorder are more likely to happen to survivors. These long-term effects can significantly affect survivors' general quality of life, including how well they do in school, their job prospects, and their overall health.

For instance, someone who has been sexually abused as a child may find it hard to keep a steady job because the stress affects their mental health and their ability to concentrate and do their job. Another problem is that they might find it hard to make and keep good relationships because the abuse made it hard for them to trust others and get close. People who have been through stress and mental pain may also abuse drugs or develop eating disorders as unhealthy ways to deal with their problems.

The long-term effects of child sexual abuse show how important it is to keep helping and supporting survivors as they become adults. By being aware of and dealing with these effects, we can help people get the tools and support they need to heal and start over with their lives.

Healing and Support

Therapy and counseling are very important for people who have been sexually abused as children to help them heal and stay mentally healthy. Therapy that focuses on trauma and support groups can help with the mental effects of being sexually abused as a child. Cognitive-behavioral therapy (CBT), eye movement desensitization and reprocessing (EMDR), and dialectical behavior therapy (DBT) are all methods that have been shown to help trauma patients deal with and heal from their experiences. Survivors can also get help, information, and tools from a wide range of groups, hotlines, and online communities as they start the process of healing.

For example, the goal of trauma-focused treatment is to help abuse survivors deal with and handle the painful memories and feelings that come with it. This kind of therapy can help people learn good ways to deal with stress, become more resilient, and feel like they have control over their lives again. Support groups give survivors a safe place to meet others who have been through similar things. These people can validate, understand, and help each other.

It's hard and takes time to heal from the long-term effects of child sexual abuse. It needs a complete and all-around method that takes into account survivors' physical, social, and mental needs. We can help people heal and take back their lives by giving them access to therapy, support groups, and other tools.

Supporting Your Child After Sibling Sexual Abuse

Sibling sexual abuse is rarely mentioned but is just as harmful as other types of sexual abuse. Parents must recognize the significant impact this may have on their children. Abuse can cause bewilderment, remorse, humiliation, and betrayal. The youngster may alternate between affection and hate toward their sibling, which can be confusing and unpleasant.

Safe and supportive environment

You are crucial to providing a secure and nurturing environment for your child. Communicate honestly to reassure your youngster that they are not responsible. Encourage children to talk and listen without judgment. Make sure they feel comfortable and affirm their feelings. You want your child to feel heard, believed, and supported.

Seeking Professional Help

Managing sibling sexual abuse is complicated and frequently requires expert help. A qualified sexual abuse mental health counselor should assist. Therapy gives kids a secure place to process emotions and acquire coping skills. Family therapy can also help you and your family comprehend sibling sexual abuse and heal.

Meeting Both Kids' Needs

Both victim and perpetrator needs must be met. Children who abuse need expert support to understand and alter their conduct. This is about identifying the causes of abuse and avoiding similar events, not assigning blame. Both kids require help with their unique habits and experiences.

Navigating Family Dynamics
Sibling sexual abuse strains families. Supporting the victim without alienating the aggressor is crucial. Setting limits and guidelines may help keep family members secure and comfortable. Open communication, family therapy, and individual counseling can help navigate these complicated interactions.

Education for You and Your Family
Prevention and comprehension depend on education. Teach your family about sexual abuse, its indicators, and its effects. Your family can prevent future abuse and assist one another through healing with this understanding. Books, courses, and support groups are helpful.

Progressing Together
Sibling sexual abuse is difficult for any family. Healing takes patience, understanding, and dedication. Rehabilitation is feasible with the correct support and initiatives. Your support, love, and dedication to resolving the issue can help your kid heal and improve your family's well-being.

Understanding the Ongoing Impact of Child Sexual Abuse
Child sexual abuse has deep and long-lasting effects on the mental and emotional health of those who have been through it. To deal with the long-term effects of child sexual abuse, it is important to make more people aware of the problem, offer full support, and step in quickly. We can help people heal and start over by knowing the long-term effects and giving them the tools and support they need.

It's important to remember that everyone's path to treatment is different, and there is no one-size-fits-all way to get better. But by encouraging understanding, kindness, and the right kind of help, we can make society better prepared to deal with the long-lasting effects of child sexual abuse and help people get better. For all children, we can work together to stop child sexual abuse, help survivors, and make the world a better and more caring place for all.

RESOURCES

- Book: "The Courage to Heal: A Guide for Women Survivors of Child Sexual Abuse" by Ellen Bass and Laura Davis: Addresses the lasting impact of child sexual abuse on women and guides healing.
- Book: "Victims No Longer: The Classic Guide for Men Recovering from Sexual Child Abuse" by Mike Lew: Focused on the long-term effects of child sexual abuse on men, providing insights and strategies for recovery.
- Book: "The Body Keeps the Score: Brain, Mind, and Body in the Healing of Trauma" by Bessel van der Kolk: Explores the broader impact of trauma, including child sexual abuse, on the body and mind.
- Article: "The Long-Term Effects of Child Sexual Abuse" by Kendall-Tackett, Williams, and Finkelhor (2008) - Journal of Child Sexual Abuse: An academic article providing a research-based exploration of the enduring effects of child sexual abuse.
- Book: "Childhood Disrupted: How Your Biography Becomes Your Biology, and How You Can Heal" by Donna Jackson Nakazawa: Explores the long-term impact of childhood trauma, including sexual abuse, on physical and mental health.
- Book: "Wounded Boys Heroic Men: A Man's Guide to Recovering from Child Abuse" by Daniel Jay Sonkin: Focuses on the long-term effects of child abuse on men and provides guidance for recovery.
- Article: "The Long-Term Consequences of Child Maltreatment: A Systematic Review of Observational Studies" by Norman G. Poythress et al. (2021) - Trauma, Violence, & Abuse Journal: A systematic review providing an overview of various observational studies on the lasting consequences of child maltreatment, including sexual abuse.

| 3 |

Why is Sexual Abuse So Hard for Parents?
Understanding the Emotional Impact, Challenges, and Support Needed

Why is Sexual Abuse So Hard for Parents?
Parents have to deal with sexual abuse all the time, which is very hard and breaks their hearts. There are many feelings, problems, and social stigmas that come with it that can make things even harder to handle. It's important to understand why these problems are happening if you want to help and understand parents who are living with the effects of sexual abuse.

Emotional Impact on Parents
Parents who find out their child has been sexually abused often feel a lot of different feelings at once. They might feel so guilty that they can't stand it because they didn't protect their child. They may feel like they've failed as parents and feel too ashamed to deal with their feelings of shame. Parents who are dealing with the wrongdoing and abuse their

child has gone through often feel angry at the person who did it and the situation.

After going through all of these feelings, parents may also have mental health problems because of the stress. Parents who have had their child sexually abused often have depression, anxiety, and post-traumatic stress disorder (PTSD). These mental problems can make it harder for them to deal with things and help their child.
Some parents may also feel sad over the time their child has lost. They might be sad about the broken trust and the harm the abuse did to their child's health. These feelings can be too much to handle, and you may need professional help to get through them.

Challenges Faced by Parents

Parents have a hard time telling when their child is being sexually abused. Children don't always tell adults right away when they're being abused, and the signs can be minor or easy to miss. This can make it take longer for help and action to reach the child, making the parents even more upset because they may feel useless and unsure how to protect their child.

Additionally, parents may feel stressed out by the formal steps needed to report the abuse. Dealing with the legal system and working with the police can be hard on the emotions, which makes things even harder for parents. Parents may also find it hard to accept that their child has been abused and get over their denial. This is because it shakes their sense of security and makes them question their thoughts about the world.

In addition, parents may have trouble getting the right help and tools for their children. It can be hard to find therapists who specialize in trauma-focused treatment and support groups for both the child and the parents. Parents may not be able to get the help they need because these services are not available in all places or because they are too expensive.

Societal Stigma and Shame

Parents of children who have been sexually abused often feel judged and stigmatized by society, which can make their mental pain worse. They could be blamed for the abuse or for not being good parents. Parents may feel alone, scared, and ashamed because of this reputation and judgment, which keeps them from getting the help they need.
Parents may not tell anyone about the abuse or get help because they are afraid of being judged and shamed. They might be worried about how other people will see them and their child and how that might change how their family works. Misconceptions and myths about sexual abuse can also make parents even more afraid, which makes it even harder for them to come forward and get help.

Society needs to fight these stereotypes and make sure that parents can talk about their problems and get the help they need in a safe and loving space. We can help parents feel less shame and alone by encouraging understanding and empathy. This will also motivate them to get the help and tools that can help them heal.

Importance of Support for Parents

Parents need to get help as they deal with the effects of sexual abuse on both themselves and their children. Professional guidance and therapy can help parents work through their feelings, understand the court system, and find ways to deal with stress. It gives them a safe place to discuss their worries, fears, and doubts.

In addition to getting help from a professional, talking to other parents who have been through the same thing can be very helpful. Online support groups and hotlines give parents a sense of community and understanding. They let parents share their stories, get help, and feel better knowing they are not alone. These sites give parents a safe and private place to talk about their thoughts and get advice from people who have been through the same problems.

Take the case of a mother who finds out that her child has been sexually abused. She feels terrible about not being able to protect her child and blames herself for that. She can talk to other parents who have been through the same feelings and problems by joining a support group. They show her compassion, understand her, and help her figure out how to deal with the justice system and find healing for herself and her child.

Support Services for Parents

Parents whose children have been sexually abused can get help from several different organizations. For example, the National Sexual Assault Online Hotline helps parents for free and in private. Support specialists who have been trained give advice, tools, and connections to help people heal and improve. Parents in trouble can call the Online Hotline anytime, day or night, for instant help.

For example, a father who is having a hard time dealing with the mental effects of his child's sexual abuse will ask for help. He talks about his feelings of guilt, anger, and shame in therapy meetings where he is safe. He learns good ways to deal with his problems and gets a better idea of how to help his child improve through therapy.

Long-Term Consequences for Parents

Parents who were sexually abused as children may have physical, mental, and social effects that last a long time. When they hear that their child is being abused, the bad things that happened to them as a child may come back to the surface. They might have problems with their close relationships and trouble being parents. Traumatic events in their own lives can make it harder for them to give their child a safe and caring home.

People who have been sexually abused as children may also abuse drugs or use unhealthy ways to deal with their problems. They can make it harder for parents to help their children get better while using these harmful ways of living. Parents need to deal with their trauma and get help from therapists who are trained to work with trauma in order to break the cycle of trauma and give their children the best care possible.

Healing and Prioritizing Self-Care

Parents must put their health and self-care first to help their children. Parents can deal with their stress and learn healthy ways to cope by working with therapists who are trained to do so. These experts can help parents deal with the complicated feelings that come up because of the abuse and help them become stronger.

Individual counseling meetings tailored to parents' needs. These meetings are mostly about dealing with the mental effects of abuse, learning how to take care of yourself, and helping people heal. Parents can better help their children and make the family unit healthy if they care for their health.

How to Stop the Cycle of Trauma

Sexual abuse as a child can lead to more pain and abuse as an adult. Parents who have been abused may be more likely to get into harmful situations as adults. Getting caught in this loop can make it hard for them to give their children a safe and caring home.

Parents who want to break the cycle should get legal help to protect their children and use their rights. This could mean getting protection orders, asking for changes to custody, or defending themselves against charges that they can't parent their children well. When parents take these steps, they can make their homes safer for their children and reduce the chance they will become victims again.

How to Respond to Reports of Abuse

When a child tells their parents about sexual abuse, they need to be supportive, quick to reply, and sensitive. It's important to believe and validate the child's story since children don't often lie about things that happened to them that were so scary. Parents should soothe and support the child and tell them that the abuse is not their fault.

Parents can get helpful information about what to do next and what tools are available by calling helplines and talking to experts. These tools can help you find the right therapists, get help with the court system, and access community resources. To ensure the child is safe and healthy, you must act quickly and with knowledge.

In Breaking Barriers: Moving beyond sexual abuse causes parents a lot of problems, both mentally and physically. Parents have a hard time dealing with sexual abuse because of the mental effects, the fact that it can be hard to see and accept the abuse, social guilt and shame, and the fact that support services are very important. Parents need to get help, put their healing first, and stop the cycle of stress to help their children.

Parents can heal and get better with the help of specialized therapy and support. By pushing parents to get help and giving them the tools they need, we can help them get through the challenging healing process and give their children the best care possible.

RESOURCES

- Book: When Your Child Has Been Molested: A Parent's Guide to Healing and Recovery by Kathryn B. Hagans and Joyce Case Potter: Offers guidance for parents on navigating the emotional challenges and supporting their child's healing process.
- Book: Beyond Betrayal: Taking Charge of Your Life after Boyhood Sexual Abuse by Richard B. Gartner: Focuses on the impact of sexual abuse on men and their families, addressing the challenges faced by parents.
- Book: Trauma-Proofing Your Kid: A Parents' Guide for Instilling Confidence, Joy and Resilience by Peter A. Levine and Maggie Kline: Explores strategies for parents to help their children build resilience and cope with trauma, including sexual abuse.
- Darkness to Light (d2l.org): Provides resources and information for parents on preventing child sexual abuse and understanding its impact.
- Rape, Abuse & Incest National Network (RAINN) - Parents (rainn.org): Offers guidance for parents on supporting their child after sexual assault, as well as resources for parents themselves.
- Stop It Now! (stopitnow.org): Focuses on preventing child sexual abuse and provides resources for parents on recognizing and responding to concerning behaviors.
- The Impact of Child Sexual Abuse on Parents: A Literature Review and Conceptual Model by Megan R. Holmes et al. (2016) - Trauma, Violence, & Abuse Journal: An academic article exploring the emotional impact on parents and proposing a conceptual model for understanding their experiences.
- Parents' experiences of childhood sexual abuse disclosure: A systematic review of the literature by Carrie Anne Marshall et al. (2021) - Child Abuse & Neglect Journal: Examines the challenges parents face when their child discloses sexual abuse and the support needed.
- Child Welfare Information Gateway (childwelfare.gov): Offers resources on child abuse prevention, intervention, and support for parents.
- NSPCC - Supporting Parents (nspcc.org.uk): The National Society for the Prevention of Cruelty to Children provides information and resources to support parents dealing with child abuse.

Journey to Healing:

| 4 |

The Emotional Journey: Understanding and Healing the Toll of Sexual Abuse

Abuse of children can hurt their parents' feelings.
Parents who have had a child affected by sexual abuse often feel many things, such as anger, guilt, fear, and loneliness. Parents may feel too sensitive to handle if you tell them about something so upsetting. Most of the time, mothers whose children have been sexually abused are less happy with their parenting, have more mental health issues, and have families that don't work, as well as mothers whose children have not been sexually abused.

Source: https://pubmed.ncbi.nlm.nih.gov/8958459

Let us look at the case of a mother who learns that her child has been sexually abused. Because she didn't protect her child, she may feel so bad that she can't stand it. She may feel angry at both herself and the person who hurt her child, and she may also worry about her child's safety. She might also feel lonely and alone because she might be ashamed or guilty of talking to other people about the abuse.

When parents hear that their child is being sexually abused, they may also feel helpless and used. They might not think they can keep their child safe and feel like they've done a terrible job. The idea that parents have a job to protect their children and that they should always be able to do so can make these feelings worse. It can be very hard for parents to deal with all of this stress, which can be bad for their health.

What it does to your mental health and well-being

Parental sexual abuse can have a big impact on their mental health and well-being. When parents find out their child has been sexually abused, they might have mental health issues and find it hard to let go. Thoughts like worry, sadness, and PTSD may appear after going through it. These effects on the mind can last a long time, and you might need professional help and advice.

Parental worry about sexual abuse can make them feel very bad about their mental health. Some signs that a parent is anxious are thinking a lot, getting antsy, and having trouble focusing. Also, they might be depressed if they are always sad, lose interest in things they used to enjoy and feel like they don't belong. Post-traumatic stress disorder (PTSD) can happen to parents who see their child being sexually abused.

Some signs of PTSD are having unpleasant thoughts, flashbacks, dreams, and being too alert all the time. Some parents may have these mental health issues, which can really hurt their health and general well-being. Parents should be aware of how this makes them feel and get the treatment and help they need. Some people find it hard to be a parent, but therapy and counseling can help them learn how to deal with their issues and emotions healthily. Weakness is not a reason not to get help from anyone. Instead, it's a good step toward getting better and healing.

Wanting to get help and therapy

A parent who has a child who has been sexually abused needs to get help and therapy right away. A professional can help parents deal with the mental toll and be there for them as they heal. Therapists and counselors who work with stress can help parents figure out how to handle and work through their feelings.

Don't forget that getting better takes time and that you need help from someone else. Outside help may be needed to deal with the mental effects of sexual abuse on the whole family since the effects can go beyond the parent who was abused. For instance, a mom might need one-on-one therapy to deal with her anger and guilt. The family might be able to trust each other again, talk to each other better, and feel safe and loved at home again after therapy. Parents who go to therapy can talk about how they feel, get a better sense of what's going on, and learn healthy ways to handle things. With this skilled help, parents can begin to heal and feel in charge of their lives once more.

There are more ways for parents to help than just going to therapy. Parents can talk about their problems in a safe space with other parents who have been through the same things. They can also learn from each other's ways of handling things. These groups can be run by professionals or put together by people in the same neighborhood. Websites and chat rooms for parents can also help and support each other and let parents talk to each other.

Phone lines and groups for parents

There are parent support groups and other places where people who have been sexually abused can get help. Meeting people who have been through the same things as you can help you feel understood and accepted. It's safe for parents to talk about their feelings in support groups. They can also learn new things and find new ways to deal with issues. These groups can be run by professionals or put together by people in the same neighborhood. There are also online boards and groups where parents can meet other people who have been through the same things.

Someone in a parent support group might have been through the same thing as you—their child was sexually abused. Members of this group can talk about their lives, help each other, and learn from how each other troubleshoots. Friends and family who understand can help parents get better by letting them know they are not alone and that there is hope for healing.

Other than support groups, there are many other places where parents who have been sexually abused can get help. Websites, books, and papers can help you learn new things and figure out how to solve issues. Parental tools like these can help them understand how they feel and get through the healing process. When a parent goes through the mental pain of their child being abused, they should remember that they are not alone and that others can help them.

How to Handle Stress as a Parent

There are many ways for parents who have been sexually abused to deal with their feelings. Take care of yourself by doing hobbies or learning how to rest. This will help parents deal with stress better. To get support and direction, it can be very helpful to get professional help, like therapy or counseling. Having a network of trusted family and friends can also be very helpful for your mental and physical health. Parents want to help their children get better and look out for their health.

One way for parents to deal with worry might be to recharge by doing things that make them happy or getting some rest. Some things that can help with this are writing, reading, and spending time outside. To deal with the mental effects of sexual abuse, it can also be very helpful to get help from a professional. Parents can learn how to deal with their thoughts and problems by seeing a doctor or psychologist. In the end, making friends and family can give parents a sense of community and help when things get tough. Aside from giving you real help, people you trust, like family and friends, can listen and help you through this tough time.

Don't forget that everyone deals with stress in their unique way. What works for one mom might not work for another. To get rid of stress, people need to try various methods until they discover the most effective one. They can find what makes them feel better and help them deal with their feelings well if they try different things.

How parents heal and get better through the process
Take your time, be kind, and take care of yourself if you are a parent who has been sexually abused. You can deal with your thoughts and get better by going to therapy or counseling. You should treat yourself with kindness as a parent and ask for help when you need it. Know that getting better takes time and that everyone has a different route. Parents can get through the tough mental times and get better by getting help, taking care of themselves, and learning how to cope.

People who have been sexually abused as children don't heal and get better all at once. It has both successes and mistakes, big steps forward and small steps back. Parents should treat themselves with kindness and wait for them to get better as they deal with their worries. Even though things are going slowly, each small step forward is very important. There are many emotions that parents may feel as they try to heal. Some of these are anger, sadness, and frustration. These are tough times for parents, so they need help from professionals, family and friends, and support groups.

To get better after being sexually abused, you and your child need to learn how to set healthy limits. They might have to change what they do and how they interact with their children because the pain of sexual abuse can change how they feel about them. They should be honest and open with their children and make sure they feel safe enough to talk about their thoughts and fears. Children and adults can trust each other more, talk to each other better, and feel more linked after family therapy.

Links that can help you get private help
People who have been sexually abused and want to talk about it and get help to heal and recover can call the National Sexual Assault Online Hotline. It is free and private. You can get help from trained support specialists, get tools to help you heal and get better, and make links for long-term support.

The Online Hotline is open 24 hours a day, seven days a week, for chats in both English and Spanish. There are safety measures in place to keep the Online Hotline a safe and private place to talk. Parents need to get help from people they can trust and not tell anyone about it so they can get better.

Parental support and help can be found in a safe and private space at the National Sexual Assault Online Hotline. Support specialists who have been trained know how to help parents who have been sexually abused in a kind and loving way. Either through chat or the phone, parents can get the help they need to start getting better. They can get long-term help through the Online Hotline, which puts parents in touch with workers who can help them.

Families can also get help from psychotherapists, groups, or counselors in their area who deal with sexual abuse and trauma. These professionals can help parents and their children in ways that are specific to what they want. Every tool has its pros and cons, and parents should compare them all to find the best one for their family.

What it means for parents in the long run
The mental and physical health of parents can be hurt for a long time by sexual abuse. Multiple experiences, like being sexually abused and not having family support, can lead to PTSD, sadness, anxiety, and trouble believing in other people. When parents are sexually mistreated, it can have very bad effects, and the children may need help and support for a

long time. Giving parents skilled help and support can help them get better without any long-term effects. They need to take care of their health and get the help they need to get better.

There may be a lot of trouble in the future for parents who have been sexually abused. After years have passed, parents may still have PTSD signs like having unwanted thoughts, flashbacks, and being too alert. Also, sadness and anxiety can last for a long time, which makes their quality of life worse in general.

It may also be harder for parents who have been sexually abused to trust other people, like their partners and other adults in their lives. You might also feel shame, guilt, and blame for yourself, which can make it harder to get better. If a parent has been sexually abused, they can deal with the long-term effects by getting help and staying in touch with their sources. With the help of experts and treatments that have been shown to work, parents can feel like they are in charge of their lives again. Neuropsychosocial therapy is one example. Parents should look after their sanity and health and ask friends and family for help when they need it. If parents get the right tools and help, they can rebuild and get stronger.

Parents who have been sexually abused need to know how it hurts their minds and do something about it. Get help, go to therapy, and learn how to deal with your mental health issues so that you can heal and get back to normal. Don't forget that getting better takes time and that everyone has a different path. Parents shouldn't be afraid to get help from pros, support groups, or their tools to get through this tough time. If parents get the right tools and help, they can get over what happened and become better.

Both the child and their parents are in a lot of pain and sadness after being sexually mistreated. Child sexual abuse by a parent can have a big effect on their mental and emotional health and cause a lot of emotional issues. To help parents get better and get support, it's important to understand how sexual abuse makes them feel and what kinds of coping skills can help them get through this tough time.

How sexual abuse makes parents feel

Parent's of a child who has been sexually abused often has a lot of strong emotions about it. Parental pain can be too much for some, and it can make them sick and make it harder for them to help their child. Researchers have found that mothers whose children have been sexually abused may be more mentally upset, have problems with their families, and be less happy with their parenting than mothers whose children have not been abused. Fathers whose children have been sexually abused also go through mental pain, though it's usually not as bad as it is for moms. This difference in how people feel could be due to many things, such as gender roles and social norms.

> Here is where you can get it: https://pubmed.ncbi.nlm.nih.gov/8958459

Just think about a mother who finds out that her child has been sexually abused. That's how hard it is on them. She is angry, guilty, scared, and powerless, among other things. The mother is mad because someone hurt her child and broke their trust. When a mother can't protect her child or doesn't see the signs of abuse right away, she may feel bad, which can make her even more angry. Fear grips her as she strives to keep her child safe and sound. She has no idea what will come next.

Sometimes, moms feel hopeless when they know they can't change what happened or make their child feel better. These feelings can be too much to handle, and parents who have been sexually abused may feel alone and separated as they try to deal with the effects of the abuse.

Things that parents often think and feel

People whose children have been sexually abused often have a lot of different emotions that come and go. Along with the anger, guilt, fear, and helplessness we already talked about, parents may also feel sad, ashamed, confused, and misled. Parental feelings like these can be too much for some, and they may find it hard to go about their daily lives. This is something that parents need to be aware of and talk to their children about so that they can deal with and heal.

Like, a parent might be very sad when they learn that their child has been sexually abused. They might be sad because they feel bad about the hurt their child has been through and the fact that their child is no longer good. Another reason they might feel bad is that they think they failed to protect their child.

Parents may also feel confused as they try to understand how this could happen to their child and why the attacker would do this. When a parent finds out that someone, they trusted broke their child's trust, they may have lied to them. It can be hard for parents to heal because these feelings can be confusing and at odds with each other.

How to Handle Stress as a Parent
You can't handle the mental effects of sexual abuse on your own. You need help and tools. Parents whose children have been abused need to learn how to handle their feelings and the issues that arise as a result. Parents whose children have been sexually abused need to get help and support right away from a professional.

Making a safety plan for the family can also help parents dealing with sexual abuse feel safe again and in charge. Building plans are in this plan to keep the child safe from more harm and make sure they are healthy. For example, you could keep a closer eye on their child, set limits, and teach them how to stay safe around their bodies. Making a safety plan is one way for parents to help keep their children safe.

Think about a parent who goes to therapy to deal with the mental effects of being sexually abused as an example of another way to solve a problem. Parents can talk about how they feel, get a better sense of what's going on, and learn healthy ways to deal with stress in a safe and helpful setting by going to therapy. Therapists who specialize in trauma and sexual abuse can help parents work through their feelings and figure out how to best help their children while they heal.

Support groups are also helpful because they let parents talk to other parents who have been through the same problems and share their stories. Parents can also lower their stress and improve their health by doing things like sports, exercise, or relaxation. This will help them be better parents for their children.

The process of parents getting better

Parents whose children have been sexually abused need time, kindness, and help to learn how to get better. People who have been sexually abused as children can get over their feelings with the right care and help.

A lot of children need help from people who care about them to get better without any long-term effects. Our goal is to stop sexual abuse before it happens and to talk about it freely. We should also teach children about body safety and healthy boundaries.

Adult children should take care of themselves, get help from people they know, and join support groups while they are getting better. As part of taking care of yourself, you can do things that make you happy and calm down, like going outside, practicing mindfulness, or having hobbies. Parents need to remember to take care of themselves and give themselves time to rest and get better when they have children.

Some parents find it helpful and comforting to talk to other parents who have been through the same things. Parents whose children have been sexually abused can feel safe in support groups where they can talk about what happened, learn new things, and get help. People in these groups have been through the same thing and can learn from each other.

They can also get help and understanding from people who know how sexual abuse makes parents feel.

When their child has been sexually abused, parents need a lot of help to get through it. As parents, you should get help for yourself because you often have to carry your child's pain. It can be hard on their minds, but seeing a therapist or counselor from outside the family can help them deal with it and speed up the healing process. These people know how to deal with worry and can help and give advice to parents that is right for them.

Along with professional support, parents can get information and help from helplines and groups that are dedicated to helping people who have been abused. Stop it now! A service, for instance, lets people who are afraid about sexual abuse of children get help and advice without being seen. They can tell you how to deal with abuse and help you find help and tools to heal. Parents can help stop and deal with abuse by giving money to groups that work to protect children and help people who have been sexually abused.

Families that want to learn and get help can also use books and other learning tools. Parents who read books about sexual abuse can talk to their children about what is and isn't okay to do and get tips on how to help their children get better. Someone afraid of child sexual abuse can get help from the Lucy Faithfull Foundation. They offer advice and support in a safe space. They give parents a lot of information and tools to help them learn more about how to help their children who have been sexually abused.

What it means for parents in the long run
The parents of children who were sexually mistreated may have issues with their physical and mental health as adults, as well as with how they act sexually. Parental PTSD, sadness, worry, and trouble trusting people are all things that can happen. Parents who were sexually abused may

have health problems that last a long time and make it hard for them to make close friends and family. This can lower their quality of life in general.

When these things happen, parents need to put their health first and get help from a professional. To lessen the long-term effects of sexual abuse on parents, they need to get help that works and keep getting care. Assisting parents through trauma can get the help and direction they need to deal with their emotions in a healthy way and start over.

How it changes the relationship between a parent and child
Sexual abuse can make it hard for a parent to connect with their child. When children are sexually abused, it can be hard for them and their parents to get along with each other. If you want to have a good bond with your child, you need to rebuild trust. It's important to be open and honest with your child if you want them to feel safe and loved.

Therapy is a good way to fix and make the relationship between a parent and child better. Giving each parent and child their therapy can help them feel safe enough to talk about how they feel, figure out what happened, and get better. Another thing that can help is family therapy, which lets everyone talk to each other easily and helps the family trust and understand each other again. The more parents go to therapy, the better they can learn how to talk to their children, set good rules, and help their children heal.

When people want to stop the sexual abuse of children, they need to push for changes in society who are parents. Parents learning how to stop abusing their children and themselves is a big part of making a place safe. Teach your child about body safety, approval, and healthy limits. This will give them the tools to protect themselves and spot signs of abuse. There are tools and programs for protection that can help parents do their job by teaching them how to spot and report abuse.

Being a champion can mean a lot of different things. For example, you can talk about how important it is to have full sex education or give money to groups that work to stop child sexual abuse. To make the world a better place for children, parents should share knowledge, question social norms, and ask for changes to laws and rules.

Parents need to know how sexual abuse makes them feel so they can get help and heal. A lot of the time, parents whose children have been sexually abused feel very angry, guilty, scared, and helpless. You should get professional help, learn how to handle issues and look for help for yourself.

Parents can get better and start over by taking care of their mental health. To make the world a better place for children, it's also important to push for change and safety. As we work to make the world a place where sexual abuse doesn't happen, we can help parents and people who have been sexually abused.

RESOURCES

- Book: The Courage to Heal: A Guide for Women Survivors of Child Sexual Abuse by Ellen Bass and Laura Davis: Addresses the emotional journey of healing for women survivors of child sexual abuse.
- Book: Beyond Survival: A Guide to Healing from Childhood Sexual Abuse by Maureen Brady: Explores the emotional challenges survivors face and provides guidance on the path to healing.
- Book: The Body Keeps the Score: Brain, Mind, and Body in the Healing of Trauma by Bessel van der Kolk: Examines the impact of trauma, including sexual abuse, on the body and mind and offers insights into the healing process.
- RAINN (rainn.org): The Rape, Abuse & Incest National Network offers resources and information on healing from sexual abuse.
- Joyful Heart Foundation (joyfulheartfoundation.org): Focuses on healing and empowerment for survivors of sexual assault, providing resources for the emotional journey.
- Pandora's Project (pandys.org): An online community and resource center for survivors of sexual abuse, offering support and understanding.
- The Healing Journey for Male Survivors of Childhood Sexual Abuse by David Lisak and Paul M. Miller (2002) - Journal of Interpersonal Violence: An academic article discussing the unique emotional journey of male survivors and the challenges they may face.
- Understanding the Impact of Child Sexual Abuse: Implications for Family Court Decision Making by Christine Wekerle and Sarah L. Whitfield (2017) - Journal of Family Violence: Explores the emotional impact of child sexual abuse on families, including the legal and court-related aspects.
- MaleSurvivor (malesurvivor.org): Specifically tailored for male survivors of sexual abuse, offering resources and support for their emotional journey. National Sexual Violence Resource Center (NSVRC) - Healing (nsvrc.org): Provides resources on healing after sexual violence, including articles and guides on the emotional toll.

| 5 |

Understanding Legal Obligations in Cases of Child Sexual Abuse:
Reporting, Consequences, and Support

Sexual abuse of children is a horrible crime that has terrible, long-lasting effects on the children who are abused. To protect children's safety and well-being, it is important to know what the law requirements are for reporting child sexual abuse. Reporting these crimes quickly and correctly is crucial to stop more harm and hold the criminals responsible.

Different places have different laws about how to report sexual abuse of a child, but there are some rules and duties that are the same everywhere. Anyone who knows or has a good reason to think that a child under 18 is being sexually abused must report it right away to the police or the child protection body in charge. People who are 18 years or older are required to do this.

Some workers, called "mandated reporters," are forced by law to report child abuse or neglect while they see it. People who are required to report include school leaders, teachers, medical staff, social service workers, and police officers. They are required by law to report if they know or think that a child is being neglected, abused, exposed to domestic violence, in immediate danger of being abused, has a parent who can't care for them, is regularly exposed to illegal drugs, or is a victim of sexual abuse, human trafficking, or injury that wasn't caused by an accident.

If you don't report child sexual abuse, bad things can happen. The exact punishments may be different in each area, but they may include fines, jail time, or both. When working for certain groups, people who are required to report child abuse must also tell the leader of those groups about the potential abuse, and the leader must then report it to the police.

Legal Obligations for Reporting Child Sexual Abuse
When a child is sexually abused, people are legally required to follow specific rules. Legally, anyone who knows or has a good reason to think that a child under 18 is being sexually abused must report it right away to the police or the child protection office in charge. People who are 18 years or older have this duty.

Mandatory reporters, like school officials, teachers, social service workers, and police officers, are required by law to report any suspicions of child abuse or neglect. By law, they have to report if they know or think that a child is being neglected, abused, exposed to domestic violence, in immediate danger of being abused, has a parent who can't care for them, is regularly exposed to illegal drugs, or is a victim of sexual abuse, human trafficking, or injury that wasn't caused by an accident.

Some organizations require mandatory reporters to tell the leader of those organizations about any suspicions of child abuse. The leader then has to report it to the police. This method for reporting at different levels helps make sure that cases of sexual abuse of children are properly dealt with and looked into.

There can be severe penalties if you don't follow the law and report child sexual abuse. Depending on the region, people who don't report may be fined, put in jail, or both. These punishments are meant to stop people from doing bad things and stress how important it is to report child sexual abuse quickly and correctly.

People who are responsible for the sexual abuse of children should know what the law says they must do and do it as best they can. Reporting potential abuse is a very important way for people to help protect children and bring abusers to justice.

Reporting Procedures and Protocols
The proper officials give clear instructions on how to report cases of child abuse and neglect. These rules help make sure that reports are filled out correctly and quickly and that the child is protected by taking the proper steps. Different reporting processes stress the importance of telling the proper police or county child safety agencies about the problem.

One important thing you need to report child abuse or neglect is "reasonable suspicion." People must have facts or observations that make a logical person think they are being abused or neglected. People in the community, school staff, managers, coaches, and volunteers must report any suspected abuse or neglect to the proper authorities. They play a vital part in keeping children safe.

People need to learn about the standards and processes for reporting that apply to their area. By following these tips, people can make sure that reports of sexual abuse of children are made quickly and correctly, which will protect and help the victims.

U.S. National Sexual Assault Hotline (Available 24 hours)
1-800-656-4673

Consequences for Failing to Report
Not telling anyone about the sexual abuse of a child is a significant crime that can lead to legal trouble. Different places may have different punishments, including fines, possible crime charges, and other legal effects. It is very important for people who are required to report things to know that they have the right to privacy and can't be sued when they do so in good faith. These rights make people more likely to follow the law without worrying about getting in trouble.

Child safety and law enforcement agencies in your area are responsible for looking into child abuse or neglect reports and taking the proper steps. Child Protective Services (CPS) is often the primary group that steps in to stop cases of child abuse and neglect. These groups work hard to ensure that children are safe and healthy and give victims and their families the help and services they need.

People need to know what could happen if they don't report child sexual abuse. People can help protect children and stop more harm by following the required law.

Child Protection Laws and Regulations
Child protection laws and regulations vary between jurisdictions, but they all share the common goal of safeguarding children from abuse and neglect. Mandatory reporting laws require specified individuals, such as teachers, healthcare professionals, police, and religious ministers, to report suspected child abuse and neglect to authorities. The types of abuse and neglect that must be reported may differ, but they generally include physical abuse, sexual abuse, emotional abuse, neglect, and exposure to family violence.

Confidentiality and immunity from legal liability are provided to mandated reporters to encourage reporting and protect their identities. These safeguards ensure that individuals can fulfill their legal obligations without fear of personal repercussions.

Individuals must familiarize themselves with the child protection laws and regulations specific to their jurisdiction. By understanding these laws, individuals can ensure that they are fulfilling their legal obligations and contributing to children's overall protection and well-being.

Help and Resources for Survivors and Victims

People who have been sexually abused as children or who have survived it need help and tools to get better. Many different groups and organizations help and advise these people in the best ways for them. Making sure people feel safe and supported is very important if you want them to come forward and get help.

Trained experts, like counselors and therapists, are very important when it comes to figuring out if a crime has happened and giving the right help and support. These people know how to help victims through the court process and put them in touch with the right tools.

Support services and tools for victims and survivors of child sexual abuse can be found through groups that work to stop it. These groups help people deal with the complicated issues that come up after being abused by providing a variety of services such as counseling, legal help, lobbying, support groups, and therapy.

People who have been sexually abused as children can heal and get better if they have access to a wide range of support and tools.

Journey to Healing:

When a child is sexually abused, it is very important to listen to what the child has to say and then tell the police. Professionals trained can best tell if a crime has been committed or if help is needed. Continuous training and knowledge about how to spot and report child abuse and neglect are essential for people in many jobs, such as teachers, healthcare workers, and community members. Everyone can work together to stop and deal with child sexual abuse by following the law.

To sum up, knowing your legal responsibilities when reporting child sexual abuse is important for keeping children safe and taking care of this serious problem. Reports must be made quickly and correctly to protect vulnerable children, processes, and protocols must be followed, and people know what will happen if they don't say something. Society can play a big part in helping victims and survivors heal and get better by giving them support and resources. People and groups need to work together to follow the law and make the world safe for children.

RESOURCES

- Child Welfare Information Gateway (childwelfare.gov): Provides comprehensive information on legal obligations, reporting requirements, and resources for individuals involved in child welfare.
- Darkness to Light (d2l.org): Offers resources on mandatory reporting laws and guidelines, helping individuals understand their legal obligations in cases of child sexual abuse.
- RAINN (rainn.org): Includes information on legal aspects, reporting procedures, and the consequences perpetrators may face in cases of child sexual abuse.
- Legal Consequences of Child Sexual Abuse - National Sexual Violence Resource Center (NSVRC) (nsvrc.org): A comprehensive guide discussing the legal ramifications of child sexual abuse and the steps involved in reporting.
- Mandatory Reporting of Child Abuse and Neglect - Child Welfare Information Gateway (childwelfare.gov): An article providing an overview of mandatory reporting laws in the United States, outlining the legal obligations of individuals.
- Legal Obligations in Reporting Child Sexual Abuse: A Guide for Professionals - American Professional Society on the Abuse of Children (APSAC) (apsac.org): Offers guidance for professionals on their legal obligations in reporting child sexual abuse and the subsequent legal processes.
- Child Maltreatment: An Introduction by Cindy L. Miller-Perrin and Robin D. Perrin: Provides insights into the legal aspects of child maltreatment, including sexual abuse, and the obligations of individuals involved.
- Child Abuse and Neglect: A Clinician's Handbook by Suzanne S. Sgroi: Explores the legal and clinical aspects of child abuse, helping professionals understand their legal responsibilities.
- National Children's Alliance (nca-online.org): Offers information on legal advocacy for child abuse victims, including resources for professionals and individuals involved in reporting.
- Childhelp (childhelp.org): Provides legal resources and information on reporting child abuse, along with support services for those involved in the process.

Journey to Healing:

| 6 |

Identifying and Addressing Signs of Sexual Abuse in Children:
A Guide for Parents and Caregivers

Sexual abuse of children is a very bad problem that needs our attention and action. To protect children and give them the help they need, it is important to know the signs and symptoms of sexual abuse in children. This chapter will discuss some of the most common signs of sexual abuse, what to do if you think your child has been abused, how to stop sexual abuse, and tools and help for parents who are dealing with this problem.

How to Tell If Your Child Has Been Sexually Abused
It's essential to know the signs and symptoms of sexual abuse so that help and action can happen quickly. It's important to remember that these signs may look different in different children based on age and personality. When you see these signs, you should be careful:

Sexually Transmitted Infections (STI's), injuries or bruises that you can't explain, or damage to the genital area are all physical signs of sexual abuse. These physical signs should make you suspicious and want to investigate it more.

As an example, a child with an STI could be a sign of sexual abuse and should be reported. A medical worker must look at the person to determine what caused the sickness and provide proper care.
https://www.rainn.org/articles/warning-signs-young-children

Behavioral Signs: Children who have been sexually abused may change the way they act in specific ways. There's a chance that they talk too much or know too much about sexual topics for their age. They may also regress in ways, like wetting the bed, sucking their thumb, or holding to caregivers.

It can also be a red flag if someone keeps secrets or acts very private. If a child starts doing backward behaviors like thumb-sucking or wetting the bed again after growing out of them, for example, that child may be experiencing the effects of sexual abuse. It is important to talk to the child about these behavior changes and support them.

Signs of Abuse: Sexual abuse can have a big effect on a child's mental health. Watch out for changes in how they eat, mood swings, rapid attitude changes, or actions that hurt themselves. Children who have been sexually abused may also show more fear or worry.

For instance, a child who suddenly develops an eating problem or starts cutting or burning themselves may be trying to deal with the pain of being sexually abused. In these cases, offering mental support and getting professional help is very important.

Signs that a young child is being sexually abused
If a young child has been sexually abused, they may show certain warning signs. You should be careful and keep an eye out for these signs: Trust your gut and keep an eye out for quick changes in how people act.

If a child who used to be friendly and sure of themselves all of a sudden starts to be shy and scared, it could be a sign of sexual abuse. Keep an eye out for any big changes in behavior, and if you need to, get professional help. Adults may be hurting children if they don't follow limits, touch children without permission, or spend too much time alone with them. For instance, if an adult repeatedly breaks a child's personal limits, touches them inappropriately, or demands to be alone with the child for no good reason, this should be a red flag. You should follow your gut and do what you need to do to keep the child safe.

When a child is sexually abused, it can have a big effect on their mental health. Watch out for these signs of weakness:
- Anxiety, sadness, trouble sleeping, changes in eating habits, being afraid of certain people or places, mood swings, acting out or pulling away
- For example, a child who has a lot of worry, sudden mood swings, or pulls away from friends and hobbies may be showing signs of mental distress caused by sexual abuse. Giving the child a safe and caring place to live is very important for helping them deal with these mental problems.

There are different ways that physical signs of sexual abuse can show up. Pay close attention to these body signs:
- Cuts, bruises, rubs, swelling, and bumps or scabs around the mouth, pelvic area, or anus.
- If a child comes in with injuries or physical damage that can't be explained in these areas, it should make you think about sexual abuse.
- To ensure the child is safe and healthy, getting medical help and telling the right people about your concerns is very important.
- STDs, urinary tract infections, or pain that won't go away when you go to the bathroom or urinate.

These outward signs could be signs of being sexually abused. Talking to a doctor or nurse is important to determine what's causing these symptoms and ensure the child gets the proper care.

Find help at https://www.d2l.org/get-help/identifying-abuse

Teenagers' Warning Signs of Sexual Abuse

Teenagers who have been sexually abused may show and act in different ways. Keep an eye out for the following signs:

- Feelings like anger, headaches, or stomachaches that don't have a medical cause; having trouble with relationships; having low self-esteem; or not being sure of your sexual identity.
- Teenagers who have been sexually abused may have problems with their feelings and show signs of sadness. Making sure they feel safe and supported so they can talk about their thoughts and get help if they need it is important.
- Changes in behavior, such as changes in how you look, engaging in sexual or drug-abusing behaviors that are risky, or spending too much time online.
- When teens have been sexually abused, they might do dangerous things to deal with their pain. To deal with these changes in behavior, it is important to offer support without judgment and get professional help.
- Signs on the body include heat or swelling in the genital area, trouble walking or sitting, and bruising on soft body parts.
- Teenagers' physical signs should not be ignored because they could be signs of sexual abuse. Ensuring the teenager is safe and healthy means getting them medical help and telling the right people about what's happening.

"Signs of Child Sexual Abuse" can be found at
https://raisingchildren.net.au/school-age/safety/child-sexual-abuse

How to Talk to Your Child About Sexual Abuse

When talking to your child about sexual abuse, it's essential to make sure they feel safe and open to talking about it. Here are some ways to start these kinds of conversations:

From a young age, encourage your child to talk to you freely. Make them feel at ease so they can talk to you about their feelings, thoughts, and worries. This will help build trust, which will make it easier for them to talk about anything that makes them feel bad. For instance, you can start by talking about personal limits and permission in a way that is right for their age. Your child should know that their body is theirs and that they can say "no" to any touch of their body.

Age-appropriate conversation: Make sure that the things you talk about are right for your child's age and level of understanding. When you talk about body autonomy, limits, and consent, use simple words and good examples. Teach your child that their body is theirs and that no one can touch them in a bad way without their permission. Book or picture tools that teach children about safety and limits can be used with younger children.

The images to the right can assist in discussing appropriate body parts and their names based on the developmental stage of your child.

Stressing the value of reporting:

Tell your child they should speak up if they ever feel unsafe or something doesn't feel right. Tell them you believe them and will back them up. Tell them that it's not their fault if someone hurts them and that you will look out for them. Tell them to tell an adult they trust, like a teacher, psychologist, or health care worker, about bad experiences.

Journey to Healing:

What to do if you think your child has been sexually abused
Notifying the authorities right away is very important if you think your child has been sexually mistreated.

You can do the following:
As a parent, you know your child better than anyone else. If their behavior changes quickly or you know something is wrong, you should pay attention. It's essential to trust your gut when keeping your child safe. If you have any doubts, it's better to be safe than sorry and get skilled help.
Get professional help. For advice and support, call the National Sexual Assault Hotline or a sexual assault service provider in your area. There are trained professionals at these groups who can help you figure out what to do next and give you and your child the tools you need. They can help you deal with the legal and mental parts of the situation and put you in touch with the right support services.

Tell the police what you think: If you see physical signs of abuse, like injuries to the groin area or injuries that can't be explained, you should tell the police what you think. They can start an investigation and do what needs to be done to keep your child safe. It is very important to help the police with their investigation if you want justice for your child and to stop any more harm.

How to Keep Childs from Being Sexually Abused
To keep children safe from sexual abuse, the most important thing is to stop it before it happens.

To help stop sexual abuse, here are some ideas: Teach children about their bodies, rights, and limits: Your child should learn early on that their body is theirs and they can set limits. Tell them that only people who want to keep them clean or healthy should touch their private parts and that they should never lie about getting touched. Encourage people to talk openly about their safety and limits.

Tell your child what kinds of touches are safe and not safe:

A safe touch is different from a dangerous touch. Help your child understand this. You should teach them that safe touch is nice, comfy, and polite, while risky touch is scary, confusing, or uncomfortable. Tell them to follow their gut and speak up if they feel unsafe being touched. Stress how important it is for them to say "no" to any touch that makes them feel bad.

Teach your child about healthy relationships, respect, and agreement. This will help them have good conversations and relationships. Encourage them to talk to you openly and ensure they feel safe discussing their worries and feelings. Help them learn how to be bold so they can set limits and say "no" when necessary. Also, teach them to understand and accept other people's limits.

Parents who are dealing with sexual abuse can find help and resources here.

Parents who are living with the effects of sexual abuse need help and advice. You can get help from the following:

- **National Hotline for Sexual Assault Online:** People who have been sexually assaulted can call the National Sexual Assault Online Hotline for free services like support in a safe environment, healing and recovery tools, and help to find long-term support. Survivors can go there to get help and advice in a safe and private place. Through internet chat, the internet Hotline is open 24 hours a day, seven days a week.

    Go to https://www.rainn.org/about-national-sexual-assault-online-hotline to learn more.

- **Child Advocacy Centers:** These are places where families can get help and support sensitive to stress and safe for children. These centers make it easier to look into cases of child abuse because they work together and offer services like investigative interviews, therapy, and help for families. They want to make sure that the child doesn't have to go through too much stress during the review and that they get the help they need.

Remember that you are not alone and that there are groups and professionals who can help you get through this tough time. You can use these tools to get help, advice, and access to more information.

It is very important to find and deal with signs of sexual abuse in children. We can do a lot to stop and deal with sexual abuse by being alert, keeping lines of communication open, and taking the steps needed to protect our children. Get professional help and support right away if you think your child has been sexually abused. Remember to go with your gut and do what you can to keep your child safe and healthy. We can keep our children safer and better for them generally if we all work together.

RESOURCES

- Darkness to Light (d2l.org): Provides resources and guides for parents and caregivers on recognizing signs of child sexual abuse and taking preventive measures.
- NSPCC - Signs of Child Sexual Abuse (nspcc.org.uk): The National Society for the Prevention of Cruelty to Children offers a comprehensive guide for parents on identifying signs of child sexual abuse.
- Stop It Now! (stopitnow.org): Focuses on preventing child sexual abuse and provides resources for parents to recognize and address concerning behaviors in children.
- Recognizing Child Abuse: What Parents Should Know - Child Welfare Information Gateway (childwelfare.gov): A guide for parents outlining signs of child abuse, including sexual abuse, and steps to take if abuse is suspected.
- Child Sexual Abuse: A Guide for Parents and Caregivers - American Academy of Pediatrics (aap.org): Offers insights into recognizing signs of child sexual abuse and guidance on supporting children who may have experienced abuse.
- Understanding and Recognizing Child Sexual Abuse - RAINN (rainn.org): A guide that provides information on recognizing signs of child sexual abuse and offers support for parents and caregivers.
- Protecting the Gift: Keeping Children and Teenagers Safe (and Parents Sane) by Gavin de Becker: Covers a range of safety issues for children, including recognizing signs of abuse and practical advice for parents.
- The Safe Child Book: A Commonsense Approach to Protecting Children and Teaching Children to Protect Themselves by Sherryll Kraizer: Offers practical guidance for parents on teaching children personal safety and recognizing signs of abuse.
- Stewards of Children - Darkness to Light (d2l.org): An evidence-informed training program for adults, including parents and caregivers, on recognizing and responding to child sexual abuse.
- Prevent Child Abuse America (preventchildabuse.org): Provides resources for parents on preventing child abuse, including information on recognizing signs of abuse in children.

Journey to Healing:

| 7 |

Preventing Child Sexual Abuse: A Comprehensive Guide for Parents and Caregivers

A lot of children all over the world are affected by child sexual abuse, which is an unfortunate problem. As parents and other adults who care for children, it is our job to keep them safe and make sure they have an excellent place to grow and develop. It is estimated that one in ten children in the United States will be sexually abused before they turn 18. These scary numbers make it clear that we need effective protection measures right away.

Child sexual abuse is common and can have effects that last a long time for the victims. Parents and other adults who care for children need to take action to stop child sexual abuse and make sure children have a safe place to grow up. Parents and other adults who care for children can do a lot to protect them and lower their risk of being abused by using the right tactics.

Studies have shown that child sexual abuse usually happens one-on-one, and 90% of victims know the person who abused them. This shows how important it is to teach children about body safety, giving permission, and setting healthy limits. Giving children the right information and skills gives them the power to keep themselves safe and get help if they feel dangerous or uncomfortable.

Importance of Open Communication
One of the most important things that can be done to stop child sexual abuse is for parents and children to be able to talk to each other freely. Giving children a safe place to talk about their worries and thoughts can help them feel strong and encouraged. Parents and other adults caring for children must build trust and listen to their worries and fears. This will make it more likely for children to tell their parents or other adults who care for them if they see or experience any kind of abuse or bad behavior.

For instance, think about a child who doesn't like how their uncle acts at family events. If the child knows their parents will protect them and help them, they are more likely to talk about their problems and ask for help. If the child is afraid of being judged or punished, on the other hand, they might not talk about how they feel, which could put them at risk for more harm.

Talking to children at the right age about body safety and giving permission is also very important to stop child sexual abuse. Parents and other adults who care for children should start conversations about limits, what kinds of touches are okay and not okay, and the idea of permission. Talking to children about these ideas will help them understand and stick to their limits when they feel uncomfortable. Using the correct physical names for body parts also gives children more confidence and helps break down the shame that comes with talking about their bodies.

Teaching Children about Body Boundaries and Consent
To stop child sexual abuse, it is vital to teach children about personal limits and how necessary permission is. Childs should be able to talk to

their parents or other adults who care for them about what kinds of touches are okay and not okay. Teaching children to tell the difference will make them better able to keep themselves safe from harm. Children should be repeatedly told that they can say "no" to any kind of unwanted touch from anyone.

A good way for parents to teach their children how to handle uncomfortable scenarios is to play pretend with them. Parents can help their children learn the confidence and skills they need to protect themselves by putting them in situations where they have to set limits and say "no." For example, a stranger giving candy or a family member breaking personal lines are both examples of this.

Additionally, adults who care for children should teach them to believe in their gut feelings. They should be able to set limits and get help if they feel unsafe or uncomfortable in a setting. Children are more likely to notice and act on possible signs of abuse if they are taught to trust their gut and feelings. Parents and other adults caring for children need to support and acknowledge their feelings and let them know that their safety and well-being are very important.

https://www.rainn.org/about-national-sexual-assault-online-hotline

Recognizing Signs of Potential Abuse

Parents and other adults who care for children need to know how to spot the signs of possible child sexual abuse. Physical signs may include bruises that you can't explain, trouble walking or sitting, or changes in how you eat and sleep. Behavioral signs may include rapid changes in behavior, being alone, or being scared. Sudden changes in mood, worry, or sadness can be emotional signs. Parents and other adults who care for children should trust their gut and get help if they think someone is being abused.

It is important to remember that every child reacts to abuse in their way, and some signs may not show up right away. Children may show a mix of physical, behavioral, and mental signs or small changes that need to be watched closely. Parents and other adults who care for children need to keep the lines of conversation open and pay attention to any changes in their behavior or health. To help you spot and deal with possible signs of abuse, getting professional help and advice from a doctor or psychologist can be very helpful.

Creating a Safe and Supportive Environment

To stop child sexual abuse, it is very important to make the surroundings safe and helpful. Childs can better understand what is expected of them and what is not okay if their family has clear rules and limits. Talking openly about emotions and feelings can help children feel safe enough to say what they need and get help when needed. For children to feel safe and protected, their parents need to have good relationships with them that are based on trust and understanding.

Having a safe and welcoming setting can also come from spending time together as a family. Parent-child relationships can get stronger by doing things together that help them bond and talk to each other freely. Parents and other adults who care for children can better understand what they are going through and be more aware of any possible signs of abuse if they are present and involved in their lives.

Parents and other adults who care for children should also be aware of the people in their lives. Avoiding situations where abuse might happen by carefully selecting workers and knowing about the people who work with the child can help. Parents and other adults who care for children can give them a safety net by keeping a list of people they trust.

Reporting Suspicions or Incidents of Abuse

It is very important to report any accusations or acts of sexual abuse of children in order to protect them and stop more harm from happening. Parents and other adults caring for children need to know how to report these problems correctly. For example, they should call the police or child safety services. Reporting it right away can help ensure the child gets the help and care they need.

For instance, if a parent thinks that their child may be sexually abused, they should call the police or child safety services in their area. The skilled professionals in these groups can look into what's going on and take the proper steps to keep the child safe. Parents and other adults who care for children can help stop child sexual abuse and hold abusers responsible by reporting fears or incidents.

Parents and other adults who care for children who may have been abused should keep any proof that could be useful in the case. This could be text conversations, emails, or real-world proof. It is also a good idea to write down any talks or notes about possible abuse. This paperwork can be used as important proof and support during the probe.

Seeking Professional Help and Support
In situations of child sexual abuse, both the child and the parents or caregivers need to get professional help and support. Parents and other adults who care for children who have been abused are not alone in their struggles. Support and advice can be found from a wide range of groups and tools. One of these is the National Sexual Assault Online Hotline, which is run by the Rape, Abuse, and Incest National Network (RAINN). People who have been sexually assaulted can call this private hotline for help, tools, and support.

Trained experts can give advice, help with healing and recovery, and point people in the direction of long-term support. Parents and other adults who care for children should get help, whether it's therapy and counseling for themselves or their children. Getting professional help can speed up the healing process and give you the tools you need to deal with problems as they come up.

Also, neighborhood support and advocacy groups and organizations can offer extra tools and help. A lot of the time, these groups offer guidance and support groups that are just right for families and children who have been sexually abused. Parents and guardians can connect with a group of people who understand what they're going through and can offer advice and support by using these tools.

Parenting Tips and Caregiver Responsibilities

Besides the above tactics, there are a number of useful tips that parents and other adults who care for children can use to stop sexual abuse. It's very important to be an active parent and know what your child may be going through. Check-in with your child often to find out about their friends, hobbies, and experiences. Keep in touch with the people in your child's life, like managers, teachers, or family friends, and know what's going on with them.

It's also important to teach children about body safety and setting healthy limits. Give children the tools they need to trust their gut and set limits when they feel uncomfortable. Learning about ways to protect and avoid child abuse can help parents and other adults who care for children spot possible signs of abuse and take the proper steps to protect their children.

Parents and other adults who care for children should also learn how to spot the signs of child sexual abuse. By learning about the physical, mental, and emotional signs, they can be more involved in spotting possible abuse and getting help. Additionally, it is very important to teach children about these signs so they know when to get help.

Media Influence and Awareness

A lot of what children see and hear about sexual violence comes from the media. People who care for children should watch what their children watch on TV and talk to their children about how sexual violence is portrayed in media and real life. Childs can better understand consent and limits and find their way around the media world if they are taught to think critically and use media literacy.

Parents and other adults who care for children can actively monitor and limit their access to information that isn't proper for their age. Parents and other adults who care for children can keep them safe from possibly harmful effects by setting limits and giving advice on how to use media in a healthy way. Parents and other adults who care for children can teach them about healthy relationships, consent, and how to behave in a respectful way by having open conversations about media material.

Also, parents and other adults who care for children need to be very aware of the risks that come with using the internet. The internet and social media sites can be used to groom and take advantage of people. It is recommended that parents learn about these platforms' privacy settings and safety features and talk to their children about staying safe online on a regular basis.

Many things can be done to stop child sexual abuse: talking to each other openly, teaching children about body boundaries and consent, making sure the environment is safe, reporting abuse, getting professional help and support, being an involved parent or caregiver, learning about child protection, and being aware of how the media affects children. Parents and other adults who care for children can do a lot to stop child sexual abuse and make sure of their safety and well-being by using these tactics and being involved in protecting children.

RESOURCES

- Darkness to Light (d2l.org): Offers a range of resources and training programs for parents and caregivers on preventing child sexual abuse.
- Stop It Now! (stopitnow.org): Focuses on preventing child sexual abuse and provides practical tools and resources for parents to protect their children.
- NSPCC - Preventing Child Sexual Abuse (nspcc.org.uk): The National Society for the Prevention of Cruelty to Children provides guidance and resources for parents on preventing child sexual abuse.
- Preventing Child Sexual Abuse: A Guide for Parents and Caregivers - Centers for Disease Control and Prevention (CDC) (cdc.gov): A comprehensive guide outlining strategies and tips for parents and caregivers to prevent child sexual abuse.
- 10 Tips for Talking to Your Childs About Sex - Planned Parenthood (plannedparenthood.org): Offers practical advice for parents on initiating age-appropriate conversations about healthy sexuality as a preventive measure.
- Talking to Your Child About Sexual Abuse - RAINN (rainn.org): A guide that provides information on how to talk to children about sexual abuse and empower them to protect themselves.
- It's MY Body: A Book to Teach Young Children How to Resist Uncomfortable Touch" by Lory Freeman: Geared towards young children, this book helps parents teach their children about personal boundaries.
- The Better Parent: A Revolutionary Way to Bring Out the Best in Your Child by Joanne Stern and Jean Penberthy: Addresses various aspects of parenting, including creating a safe environment and open communication to prevent child abuse.
- Stewards of Children - Darkness to Light (d2l.org): An evidence-informed training program for adults, including parents and caregivers, on preventing child sexual abuse.
- Circle of Grace - Prevent Child Abuse America (preventchildabuse.org): A program designed to teach children and youth about creating and maintaining safe environments.

| 8 |

Preventing Online Child Sexual Exploitation:
Strategies, Tools, and Tips to Keep Children Safe

For children, the digital age has brought new risks and threats, so keeping them safe online is very important. As children use the internet more, it's more important than ever to keep them safe from the harm and abuse they might find there. Child sexual abuse online is one of the most critical problems in this area that needs to be fixed right away. Today, we're going to talk about ways and tools that parents, guardians, and teachers can use to stop child sexual exploitation online.

Children can learn, make friends, and discover a lot of different things on the internet. But it also puts them at risk of many things, such as being sexually exploited as a child online. To protect children from being exploited and abused, it is important to understand how serious this problem is and take action. We can make the internet a better place for children to learn and grow by spreading knowledge and using effective protection methods.

Understanding Online Child Sexual Exploitation

Online child sexual exploitation is when children are abused and used for sexual gain through different websites and apps. It includes things like bullying, sextortion, and making and sending out material about sexual abuse of children. Child abusers often use grooming, a method of building trust with a child, to sexually exploit them. Sextortion is when children are forced to give up nude photos or videos that are then used to threaten them and take advantage of them even more. Making and spreading materials about child sexual abuse keeps the circle of abuse and harm against harmless children going.

When children are abused online, they often must deal with long-lasting emotional, mental, and physical effects. They might feel ashamed, guilty, or scared, which can hurt their health and growth. To stop internet child sexual exploitation, we need to deal with this problem and act.

I'm reminded of a case in which a young adult befriended a twelve-year-old child (victim) online during the COVID-19 pandemic. The friend group began while playing online games. They were located around the world. Meanwhile, the victim began talking about problems at home, and one of the group members, a young adult, traveled more than 1,300 miles on a bus with the financial assistance of online friends. He showed up in the middle of the night at the victim's home, took him to a motel, and assaulted the child. If it were not for the phone of the victim and tracking software the police would not have found them before they took another bus out of the state, the next day.

So, the National Center for Missing and Exploited Children (NCMEC) recently did a study that showed the number of cases of internet child sexual abuse has been going up over the past few years. The study showed that attackers are using social media more and more to target and trick children, which shows that more needs to be done to raise awareness and stop this from happening.

https://www.inhope.org/EN/articles/10-ways-to-prevent-child-sexual-exploitation-online

Common Online Risks and Dangers

Online, children are at risk of many bad things that can happen to them and hurt their safety and health. The chance of seeing illegal material is one of the biggest risks. There are a lot of inappropriate pictures, violent videos, and hate speech on the internet that can hurt a child's view of the world and of themselves. Being exposed to this kind of material can make people less sensitive, confused, and even more likely to copy damaging behaviors.

Additionally, harassment is a major threat to the safety of children online. Children can be harassed, embarrassed, and threatened online, which can have very bad effects on their mental and emotional health. Children who are cyberbullied may feel alone, depressed, anxious, or even have suicide ideas. Parents, teachers, and other adults who care for children must be alert and help children who may be bullied online.

Unfortunately, internet attackers are also a big danger to children's safety. Individuals in this group trick and take advantage of children for their gain by making fake profiles or claiming to be someone else. These people may do things like training to get a child to trust them and then use them sexually. The fact that children could meet online predators shows how important it is to teach them about the risks and give them the tools they need to stay safe online.

One story about a 14-year-old girl whom an online predator harmed shows how dangerous the internet can be for children. The attacker used social media to get the girl to trust him, and then he forced her to post sexy pictures. The predator then told her they would show the pictures to her family and friends if she didn't do what they wanted. This case shows how important it is to have quick and effective ways to keep children from being exploited online.

https://protectingchildren.google/

Importance of Online Safety for Children

Children need to be very careful about their internet safety because it keeps them safe from harm and abuse that they might find online. Parents, guardians, and teachers can make sure that children are safe while they discover the internet by putting online safety first. Taking good steps to keep children safe online lets them enjoy the good things about the internet while lowering the risks that come with it.

Parents and other adults who care for children are very important when it comes to keeping them safe online. They need to talk to children openly and honestly and make sure they have a safe place to talk about their worries and experiences online. It is important to set clear limits and rules for how to use the internet. This means setting limits on how much time children can spend online, what sites and apps they can use, and how they can share private information online.

Another important part of online safety is keeping an eye on what your children do online. Parents and other adults who care for their children should know what sites and apps they use, who they talk to, and what material they watch. This can be done by using parental control software or apps, checking the browser data on a regular basis, and going over the privacy settings.

Educating children about how to stay safe online is also very important. Children should know about the risks and dangers of the internet, like how to avoid being sexually exploited online, from their parents, guardians, and teachers. It is very important to teach children how to spot possible dangers, like strange behavior or improper material, and how to report them. Teaching children how to think critically can give them the power to make smart choices and keep themselves safe online.

For instance, many groups and projects work to make the Internet a safer place for children by giving them teaching materials and tools.

These tools include materials that are right for your age, interactive workshops, and online classes that teach things like how to use technology safely, keep your privacy safe, and spot online threats. By teaching children about these tools in school, we can give them the information and skills they need to stay safe online and stop children from being exploited online.

https://www.acams.org/en/training/certificates/preventing-online-child-exploitation-with-financial-intelligence-an-overview

Tips for Parents and Caregivers

Parents and other adults who care for children play a big part in keeping them safe from online child sexual abuse.

Here are some things you can do to help keep your child safe online:

1. Talk to your child in an open and honest way. Create a safe place where they can talk about their online experiences, worries, and any problems they might face.
2. Set clear limits and rules: Make rules about how to use the internet, such as how long you can spend on it, what websites and apps are acceptable, and how much personal information you can share online.
3. Keep an eye on what your children are doing online. Use parental control and blocking software and check their digital trail often to make sure they are staying safe online.
4. Teach children about internet safety: Teach children how to protect their privacy, spot possible dangers, and report any strange material or behavior.
5. Teach children how to think critically: Teach children how to think critically so they can figure out how reliable and credible online information is.

Parents and other adults who care for children can make the internet a better place for them by following these tips. This will keep children from being sexually exploited online.

Strategies and Tools for Prevention

Stopping the sexual abuse of children online needs a multifaceted approach that includes online platforms, schools, law enforcement, and lawmakers.

To stop child sexual abuse online, here are some things you can do and tools you can use:

1. Websites should make it easy for parents to find information on how to keep their children safe online. This can include details about how to set your private settings, how to report something, and where to find more help.

2. There should be lessons in schools about child sexual abuse and the dangers of being online. Including lessons that are right for their age in the school day helps them learn the skills they need to stay safe online.

3. Online platforms should put a child-centered approach at the top of their list of priorities and set up safety measures to keep children from being exploited. This can include putting in place systems for checking people's ages, rules for content control, and proactive tracking for activities that seem fishy.

4. Laws should include clear punishments to stop bad behavior and keep children safe online. Laws should be updated and strictly followed to make sure that people who break the law are held responsible and that damaging content is taken down quickly.

5. It is very important to understand the financial reasons behind child sexual abuse content if we want to stop it. By changing the underlying economic factors, like the desire for graphic content, we can stop the making and spreading of material about child sexual abuse.

For example, several groups and projects are trying to stop the sexual abuse of children online. They work with online sites to make sure that rules and features that put children's safety first are put in place.
The other goal of these programs is to teach parents, guardians, and teachers about the risks and threats children face online and give them tips on how to keep them safe.

Resources and Organizations

Online, many places and groups offer help and information on protecting children. Here are some well-known ones:

National Safer Internet Centers: These centers help children and their families deal with online dangers by running campaigns to raise awareness and providing helplines and local hotlines.

Google: Google is dedicated to stopping the sexual abuse and trafficking of children online. They work with groups like the National Center for Missing and Exploited Children to stop online child sexual abuse and make sure that their services aren't used to spread content that is sexually abusive to children.

The free online course from ACAMS is called "Preventing Online Child Exploitation with Financial Intelligence: An Overview." Using financial intelligence methods to stop online child abuse is something that this course teaches you. Families, teachers, and other adults who care for children can get helpful information and support from these groups on how to keep children safe from being sexually exploited online.

Collaboration and Industry Efforts
Technology companies, non-governmental organizations (NGOs), and other interested parties must work together to stop online child sexual abuse.

Some important steps the industry is taking in this direction are listed below:

- Technology companies like Google put a lot of money into the fight against internet sexual abuse and mistreatment of children. Private technologies, like machine learning algorithms and hash matching technology, help them find and take down child sexual abuse content on their platforms.

- Google works with businesses and non-governmental organizations (NGOs) to make tools and share technological knowledge that can be used to stop internet content that sexually abuses children. These partnerships are meant to stop the sharing of sexually abusive material about children online and keep children from being exploited. To fight child sexual abuse online, Google is an active member of groups and alliances that bring together businesses and non-governmental organizations (NGOs).

- Google gives free access to its cutting-edge technology, like the Content Safety API and the CSAI Match API, to groups that are working to stop child sexual abuse. Google helps groups that fight child sexual abuse and exploitation by giving them funds and money. To help law enforcement officers investigate internet crimes against children, they also offer training and expert fellowships. Industry leaders can use their combined technological resources and knowledge to fight online child sexual abuse through these group efforts successfully.

Child sexual abuse is so prevalent a Google News search on the term during a 24 hour December 16-17, 2023) period provided the following stories:
- Williamson County sexual assault convict 'on the run' after release before sentencing.
- Teachers' aide charged in sex act with girl at Brooklyn school - New York Daily News
- Florida prosecutor seeks death penalty for man charged with child sexual abuse.
- A teacher pleads guilty to historical child sexual abuse. And he doesn't have to spend a day in jail.
- Florida prosecutors challenge SCOTUS precedent by seeking death penalty for child sexual abuse.
- Victims of sexual abuse students have been exposed the rot in Haryana govt schools
- Manhunt continues for Georgetown man convicted of sexual assault who skipped sentencing – KVUE.
- Lee sued over alleged sexual assault | Entertainment News - WFMZ.com
- Norwich BBQ firm files for bankruptcy on eve of civil sexual assault trial.
- Man to face court charged with historic child sex abuse - SA Police
- Man from Sanford sentenced for child sexual exploitation.
- Concord PD asks public's help to ID suspect in sexual assault | Contra Costa Herald
- Church youth adviser sentenced to prison for child porn, sexual abuse of a child |
- Mom says daughter sexually assaulted, sues Boston, bus company –
- Laurel Co. Sheriff's Office arrests sexual abuse suspect - WYMT

Stopping the sexual exploitation of children online is an important and pressing job in this digital age. We can protect children and make the internet a safer place for them to grow by using tactics and tools while raising awareness. To stop internet child sexual exploitation, parents, guardians, teachers, tech companies, and everyone else need to work together.

RESOURCES

- NetSmartz (netsmartz.org): Provides resources, educational materials, and tools to help parents and caregivers teach children about online safety and prevent online exploitation.
- National Center for Missing & Exploited Children (missingchilds.org): Offers tips and resources for parents to keep children safe online, including information on recognizing potential risks.
- Common Sense Media (commonsensemedia.org): Provides reviews, advice, and resources to help parents navigate the digital world with their children, promoting safe and responsible online behavior.
- Internet Safety for Childs: A Parent's Guide - Child Rescue Coalition (childrescuecoalition.org): A comprehensive guide for parents, including tips on setting boundaries, monitoring online activities, and promoting safe online behavior.
- Talking to Childs and Teens About Social Media and Sexting - American Academy of Pediatrics (healthychildren.org): Offers guidance for parents on discussing the responsible use of social media and addressing issues like sexting.
- Protecting Children from Online Sexual Exploitation - National Children's Advocacy Center (nationalcac.org): A guide providing information on recognizing signs of online sexual exploitation and steps for prevention.
- Safer Internet Day (saferinternetday.org): Participate in events and resources provided by Safer Internet Day, which aims to promote a safer online environment for children and young people.
- Be Internet Awesome - Google (beinternetawesome.withgoogle.com): An educational program offering resources and games to teach children about online safety, including avoiding online exploitation.
- Parent Alert! How to Keep Your Childs Safe Online by Will Geddes: Provides insights for parents on understanding the online risks their children may face and implementing practical safety measures.
- Digital Citizenship in Action: Empowering Students to Engage in Online Communities by Kristen Mattson: Focused on teaching children responsible online behavior and promoting positive digital citizenship.

| 9 |

The Impact of Social-Media on Children's Mental Health:
Exploring Risks and Strategies

Social media is now an important part of our daily lives, especially for children and teens. However, the fact that so many children use social media makes people worry about how it might affect their mental health. This piece will talk about the bad effects of social media on children's mental health and ways to encourage children to use social media healthily.

Prevalence of Social Media Use Among Children
It is not a surprise that children and teens like to use social media. In fact, two out of every three US teens own an iPhone, which shows how popular computers and social media are. In terms of how much time they spend on social media, teens and young adults are the most extreme users.

> *https://childmind.org/awareness-campaigns/childrens-mental-health-report/2017-childrens-mental-health-report/smartphones-social-media*

Childs use social media a lot, and it can help them make new friends and feel less lonely. Childs can connect with their friends, share their stories, and get help through online sites. For instance, children who have just moved to a new place or school may find comfort in social media while they try to make new friends.

However, while social media can help people connect, children's mental health can suffer if they use it too much. To make sure children are safe, it's important to know the possible risks that come with using social media.

Negative Effects of Social Media on Children's Mental Health

Researchers have found a link between children's use of social media and more mental health issues, like worry, sadness, and even suicidal thoughts. Children's self-esteem and ideas about their bodies can be hurt by seeing carefully chosen and perfect pictures on social media all the time. Comparing yourself to others on social media can make you feel bad about your abilities and boost your low self-esteem.

https://www.healthychildren.org/English/family-life/Media/Pages/what-research-says-about-social-media-and-your-childs-mental-health.aspx

For example, a study found that young girls who use social media a lot are more likely to be unhappy with their bodies and have low self-esteem because they are constantly seeing celebs and leaders who have unrealistic ideas of what beauty is. When they look at these pictures, they might feel like they're not good enough, which can be bad for their mental health.

In addition, social media changes the reward areas in teens' brains, which makes them more likely to become addicted and less likely to do risky social activities. Too much time spent on social media can make mental health problems worse and make it harder to connect with people in person. This can make people less social in real life and less likely to practice their social skills.

You can find the article at https://www.ncbi.nlm.nih.gov/pmc/articles/PMC9407706

A recent study found that teens who spend more time on social media sites tend to spend less time doing real-life social activities like going to sports games, or other community activities, or just hanging out with friends. They may feel alone and isolated because they don't have as many real-life social contacts. This can hurt their social growth.

Cyberbullying and Its Impact

Cyberbullying is one of the biggest worries when it comes to how social media can hurt children's mental health. Researchers have found a link between cyberbullying and bad mental health effects, such as sadness. The bad things about social media, like harassment, affect girls more than boys.

An experiment with a group of teens, for example, found that girls are more likely than boys to be cyberbullied. This difference between men and women may be because of how and what girls and boys like to do on social media. Cyberbullying can have very bad effects, making the people who are bullied more depressed and anxious.

Children's mental health can suffer when they are constantly exposed to cyberbullying and the fear of being attacked. They might feel unsafe and worried all the time when they use social media, which can have a big effect on their mental health as a whole.

Also, over using social media all the time can mess up your sleep habits, which can lead to sleeplessness and other sleep problems. Not getting enough sleep because of social media use can hurt your mood, your ability to think and feel, your relationships, and your ability to learn. The blue light from computers and using social media all the time can mess up a child's sleep-wake cycle, making it hard for them to fall asleep and stay asleep.

A study with teens found that those who spend more time on social media are more likely to have trouble sleeping and not be able to fall asleep. Lack of sleep can have serious mental health effects on children, such as making them less focused, irritable, and unable to think clearly.

Comparison and Self-Esteem Issues

One important thing about social media is that you always see carefully chosen and perfect pictures. This kind of exposure can hurt children's self-esteem and how they feel about their bodies. Comparing yourself to others on social media can make you feel bad about your abilities and boost your low self-esteem. The unrealistic beauty standards shown on social media can make children's body image problems even worse.

For example, a study that looked at the link between using social media and being unhappy with your body image found that young girls who use social media a lot are more likely to have bad ideas about their bodies and eat in unhealthy ways. When they are constantly compared to heavily edited and filtered pictures, it can change their idea of what is "normal" or "beautiful," which can hurt their self-esteem.

It is very important to talk about these problems and help children have a good view of their bodies and self-esteem. Promoting a healthy self-image and teaching children to value themselves for more than how they look on social media can help lessen the negative effects. Childs can use social media in a healthy way if they learn about it and get help with media literacy and critical thinking.

Sleep Disturbances and Addiction

Too much time spent on social media can make it hard to sleep. One year later, teens who spend more time on their phones are more likely to have trouble sleeping and not be able to fall asleep. Not getting enough or the right amount of sleep can mess up your energy flow and make you more likely to become overweight as a child.

Also, children who spend too much time on social media may not get enough sleep, which can have a big effect on their mood, thinking, feelings, learning, and interactions. A study found that teens who spend too much time on social media can't sleep, which can make them more irritable, make it harder for them to focus, and hurt their brain function. This could hurt their grades, their ties with other children, and their general mental health.

Also, being addicted to social media is linked to a higher chance of depression and worry. The constant need for approval and interaction on social media sites can cause children to become addicted, which can hurt their mental health and general health. It is important to know the signs of social media abuse and set up plans to encourage good habits.

You can find this advice at https://www.hhs.gov/sites/default/files/sg-youth-mental-health-social-media-advisory.pdf

For instance, a study found that teens who show signs of social media addiction, like having a strong desire to use social media and having trouble controlling their use, are more likely to show signs of sadness and anxiety. Recognizing these trends and giving children the right kind of help and support can help lessen the negative effects of social media abuse on their mental health.

Strategies for Promoting Healthy Social Media Use
Setting rules and limits is very important for making sure children use social media in a good way. Children can have a good relationship with social media if you limit their screen time and encourage them to do a mix of things online and off. Having open talks with children about the pros and cons of social media can also help them make smart decisions.

For example, parents can set limits on how much time their children can spend on social media and urge them to do other things, like reading, playing outside, or sports. Parents can make sure that social media doesn't take over their children's lives by giving them clear rules and standards.

To encourage healthy social media habits, it's also important to be good examples. Parents and other adults who care for children can teach them how to behave online and use social media safely by being good examples themselves. This means showing others how to use good internet manners, keep their information safe, and think critically.

Additionally, parental participation, such as tracking and guidance, can lessen the bad effects that social media can have on children. By keeping an eye on what their children are doing on social media, parents can know what they are seeing, how they are interacting with others, and any risks they might face. Children can feel safer asking their parents for help and advice when they talk to them about their online activities on a regular basis.

Individual Differences and Parental Involvement

Different children's temperaments and physical traits can have different effects on how social media affects their mental health. Social media might more easily hurt some children, while others might be able to handle it better. A big part of reducing the bad effects of social media on children is getting parents involved. Parents can help protect their children's mental health by keeping an eye on what they do on social media and giving them advice and support.

One study found that children who have certain psychological traits, like a lot of neuroticism or low self-esteem, may be more likely to have bad things happen when they use social media. Understanding these differences between people can help parents help their children in the best way possible.

Limiting your child's social media use and being involved in it can help them develop good habits and keep them safe online. Parental support can help children feel safe talking about their online experiences and asking for help when they need it by encouraging open communication and building trust.

Social Media Use and Learning Opportunities

Some bad things could happen on social media, but it can also be used to learn and get useful material. Childs can use tools that teach them, talk to experts in different areas, and be a part of educational communities. Social networking sites can be very helpful for sparking inspiration, learning new things, and seeing more of the world.

For example, a lot of schools and other educational groups use social media to share educational material, hold virtual meetings, and help students have conversations. Social media sites also let children learn about other countries, points of view, and global problems, which helps them understand the world better.

To make sure children get a well-rounded education, it is important to make sure they mix their time on social media with other important things, like exercise and talking to real people. Parents can help their children find a good mix between online and real activities and hobbies by encouraging them to do them. Getting children involved in arts, sports, or community events can give them a sense of success, help them make friends, and give them chances to grow as people.

Potential Psychological Problems Associated with Social Media Use

Excessive social media use can contribute to psychological problems such as anxiety, low self-esteem, and addiction. The constant exposure to unhealthy and risky media messages may increase the risk of psychological issues in children. It is crucial to recognize these potential risks and take proactive steps to promote healthy habits and well-being. Studies have shown, for example, that children and teens who use social media are more likely to show signs of worry. Being on social media sites all the time, where people often show their lives in a controlled and idealized way, can make people feel inadequate and afraid of losing out. Adding to this can make worry worse and have a bad effect on mental health.

Also, being addicted to social media can make people withdraw from society and have fewer connections with people in real life. Children who depend too much on social media may have trouble making and keeping real-life friends. This can make feelings of loneliness and separation even worse.

More and more children are using social media, which makes people worry about how it might affect their mental health. Scientists have found that children who use social media are more likely to experience mental health problems like worry, sadness, and cyberbullying. Parents, guardians, and society should encourage children to use social media in a healthy way and keep an eye on how it affects their health.

Setting rules, having open talks, being a good example, and limiting social media use are all things that can help people form better habits. To lessen the bad effects of social media on children, it's important to understand how each child is different and how family involvement can affect children. We can help children's general growth and well-being by encouraging them to find a balance between using social media and other important things, like exercise and talking to real people.

We need to do more studies to fully understand the complicated link between children's use of social media and their mental health. We can make better plans and measures to protect our children's mental health in the digital age if we keep looking into the possible risks and benefits of social media.

RESOURCES

- American Academy of Pediatrics - Media and Children (healthychildren.org): Offers articles and resources for parents on managing children's screen time, including the impact of social media on mental health.
- Child Mind Institute - Social Media, Cyberbullying, and Mental Health (childmind.org): Provides insights and resources for parents on the relationship between social media, cyberbullying, and children's mental health.
- Common Sense Media - Social Media and Mental Health (commonsensemedia.org): Offers reviews, articles, and advice for parents to navigate the impact of social media on children's well-being.
- Social Media Use and Perceived Social Isolation Among Young Adults in the U.S. - American Journal of Preventive Medicine (ajpmonline.org): An academic article exploring the potential link between social media use and perceived social isolation among young adults.
- The Impact of Social Media on Children, Adolescents, and Families - American Academy of Pediatrics (pediatrics.aappublications.org): A comprehensive report discussing the potential benefits and risks of social media on children's mental health.
- Social Media and Mental Health: A Review - Cyberpsychology, Behavior, and Social Networking Journal (liebertpub.com): An academic review summarizing research on the impact of social media on mental health.
- Digital Literacy and Citizenship Curriculum - Common Sense Education (commonsense.org): Provides lessons and resources for educators, parents, and caregivers to teach children digital literacy skills, including responsible social media use.
- Digital Well-Being for Families - Google (wellbeing.google): Offers tools and resources for families to promote healthy digital habits and manage screen time.
- Screenwise: Helping Childs Thrive (and Survive) in Their Digital World by Devorah Heitner: Explores practical strategies for parents to guide their children in using technology, including social media, in a positive and balanced way.
- The Teen's Guide to Social Media... and Mobile Devices: 21 Tips to Wise Posting in an Insecure World" by Jonathan McKee: Geared towards teenagers, this book provides tips for responsible and safe social media use.

| 10 |

Taking Care of the Family:
How Cognitive Behavioral Therapy (CBT) Can Help Overcome Child Sexual Abuse

When dealing with the effects of child sexual abuse, taking care of the family is the most important thing that can be done. Cognitive behavioral therapy (CBT) is a well-known and effectively proven method that can assist children and teens in overcoming the painful effects of abuse. The goal of CBT is to help and support both the child and their family by focusing on the health of the whole family.

A trauma-informed cognitive behavioral therapy (CBT) method helps people recognize and change their negative ideas and behaviors, as well as come up with better ways to deal with stress. When it comes to sexual abuse of children, cognitive behavioral therapy (CBT) can help children and teens get over PTSD, sadness, and behavior problems. CBT tries to heal families and improve family ties by looking at how abuse affects the whole family.

Sexual abuse of a child can have very bad effects on both the child and their family that last a long time. To speed up the mending process, it's important to remember how important it is to care for and support the whole family. That's what this piece is about the role of cognitive behavioral therapy (CBT) in taking care of the family after child sexual abuse. We will talk about the main ideas and methods of cognitive behavioral therapy (CBT), how to help someone have a healthy knowledge of sexuality, how to help someone learn good coping skills, and how to help the parent or primary guardian who is not involved in the problem. Our understanding of how CBT affects family care and support can help us better understand how it can help people heal.

Understanding Cognitive Behavioral Therapy for Child Sexual Abuse

Cognitive behavioral treatment (CBT) is an organized and goal-oriented method used to help people who have been sexually abused as children deal with their mental health issues. One of the main ideas behind cognitive behavioral therapy (CBT) is to help people recognize and question their negative thoughts, learn healthy ways to cope, and change their unhealthy behaviors. Cognitive behavioral therapy (CBT) tries to give people the power and tools they need to deal with the problems that come with abuse through a joint treatment relationship.

When it comes to child sexual abuse, cognitive behavioral therapy (CBT) helps children and teens learn how to deal with problems, change bad habits and thoughts, and feel better emotionally. Children and teens can learn to recognize and change skewed beliefs and bad self-perceptions that may have formed because of abuse by working with a trained therapist. Cognitive behavioral therapy (CBT) helps people think and deal with problems in better ways by using techniques like cognitive restructuring and exposure therapy. This can help reduce the effects of PTSD and sadness.

It is important to remember that CBT is not a one-size-fits-all method. Therapists make sure that therapy fits the needs of each person and their family. Therapists can create individualized treatment plans that meet each family's worries and help them heal by learning about the unique problems they face. In the case of a child who has trouble trusting, for example, the therapist may include tasks that help the child feel safe and secure as part of the therapy sessions.

Trauma-Focused Cognitive Behavioral Therapy (TF-CBT) for Child Sexual Abuse Victims

Trauma-Focused Cognitive Behavioral Therapy (TF-CBT) offers hope and healing to child sexual abuse victims. This evidence-based treatment is designed for traumatized children and adolescents, including sexual abuse. TF-CBT helps these youth understand and overcome the painful feelings, ideas, and behaviors that commonly follow traumatic events. It attempts to equip parents with the tools to help their kid through this difficult healing process.

Each step of TF-CBT is crucial to the child's therapeutic growth. Initial efforts focus on stability and skill-building. This is about creating a secure and supportive therapeutic atmosphere. True healing requires the kid to feel safe and understood. Teaching the youngster about personal safety and appropriate limits helps restore their sense of control and security.

Psychoeducation and safety are important early TF-CBT steps. Children and parents learn about trauma's impacts. This information empowers and normalizes the child's reactions to trauma, reducing isolation and bewilderment. Many coping methods are taught and practiced. These include stress management and emotional regulation skills to assist the youngster in coping with the high emotions that commonly accompany abuse memories. The youngster may use these life skills as an adult, not simply for therapy.

Next comes story formulation and processing. In this phase, the child is encouraged to recount the experience. A child-friendly speed and compassion are used throughout this procedure. The goal is to assist the child create a cohesive trauma story to aid recovery. It helps the youngster understand and process painful memories, lessening their power over them.

At the same time, the youngster learns to recognize and reject abusive beliefs. TF-CBT treats guilt, humiliation, and self-blame in sexually abused children through cognitive processing. Reframing these beliefs helps the youngster see the event more objectively and less self-critically.

Parental engagement is another TF-CBT cornerstone. Parents receive assistance on how to support their children and handle their own emotions about the abuse. This dual approach supports the kid and family holistically.

The third phase of TF-CBT consolidates and closes gains. The kid and family are encouraged to reflect on development and solidify skills and coping methods here. The family and therapist create a strategy to sustain these improvements and address future issues.

In conclusion, TF-CBT provides a thorough, systematic, and successful treatment for child sexual assault victims. It tackles the varied effects of trauma on the child and family, preparing the path for a future where trauma is part of the kid's story but not the defining chapter.

Learning About Child Sexual Abuse and Promoting Healthy Sexual Understanding

An important part of CBT is teaching children and their families about child sexual abuse. Therapists talk to children and their families about abuse in a way that is appropriate for their age and helps them understand what healthy sexual behavior looks like. Cognitive behavioral therapy (CBT) tries to give children more power and stop abuse before it happens again by clearing up misunderstandings and encouraging a healthy view of sexuality.

Children and teens can talk about their problems and ask questions in a safe and helpful setting during cognitive behavioral therapy (CBT) meetings. Play therapy, art therapy, and stories are just a few of the ways that therapists keep children interested and help them understand the complicated problem of child sexual abuse. Therapists help children learn more about their bodies, limits, and safety by having meaningful conversations and doing fun tasks with them. CBT gives children and their families the information and skills they need to stop abuse from happening in the future by promoting healthy sexual awareness.

For instance, a therapist might use books or other visual aids that are proper for the child's age to help them understand the idea of consent during therapy meetings. They might have the child play different roles to help them get better at setting limits and saying "no" in different situations. Therapists give children the tools they need to protect themselves and make smart choices about their bodies by giving them the information and skills they need.

Developing Effective Coping Skills
One of the main goals of cognitive behavioral therapy (CBT) is to help people learn how to deal with the problems that come up after being sexually abused as a child. Coping skills are the methods and tactics people use to handle stress, keep their feelings in check, and get through tough situations. Cognitive behavioral therapy (CBT) teaches children and families ways to deal with problems so they can handle the emotional and mental effects of abuse better.

Therapists work closely with their patients to help them find and build coping skills that are best for them. Some examples of these coping skills are deep breathing, relaxation methods, writing in a notebook, doing physical activities, and asking for help from people you trust. People can learn to deal with difficult thoughts, feelings, and behaviors by using these coping skills. This will eventually make them stronger and improve their mental health.

As an example, a therapist might teach a child deep breathing or progressive muscle relaxation to help them deal with worry or panic episodes. The child can then use these skills at home or in other stressful situations to better control their feelings and feel less stressed.

Supporting the Non-Offending Parent or Primary Caretaker

When a child has been sexually abused, the parent or main helper who did not abuse them is very important to their healing. It's important to let them know you back them and give them the help they need to deal with the problems that come with abuse. CBT knows how important it is to include the parent or main helper who isn't hurting the child in the therapy process.

During therapy, therapists work with grandparents, other family members, foster parents, and adoptive parents to help and support the child. Therapists can meet the specific needs of each family member and help them heal by working with the whole family. They might teach them how to help the child, deal with their feelings, and make the home a safe and caring place for healing to happen.

For instance, a therapist might work with a parent who isn't abusing their child to help them understand how abuse affects their child and give them ways to make their home a safe and caring place for their child. Because caring for a child who has been abused can be hard on the parent's mental health, the therapist may also help them learn how to take care of themselves.

Addressing Parent-Child Communication Skills

For people who have been sexually abused as children to heal, they need to be able to talk to each other openly and clearly. CBT knows how important it is for parents and children to talk to each other better so that there is more trust, understanding, and support. CBT tries to improve family relationships and speed up the healing process by removing obstacles to conversation and encouraging healthy ways of talking to each other.

During therapy meetings, therapists help parents and children talk to each other better. They might teach people how to listen actively, talk to others in an authoritative way, and solve problems. Parents and children can learn to talk about their wants, worries, and feelings in a healthy and helpful way by using these skills. Family members who talk to each other more often can trust each other more, understand each other better, and work together better.

A therapist might lead a parent and child through a role-playing activity where they can work on listening actively and speaking clearly. They can learn to see things from each other's points of view, get better at expressing themselves, and build their relationship through this activity.

The Importance of Family Care and Support
When a child is sexually abused, family care and support are very important. A child can generally get better faster and be healthier if they live with a caring family. Families can make a safe place for their children to feel valuable and supported by showing love, understanding, and acceptance.

A child's healing process can be helped in many ways by living in a supportive home setting. Having a sense of stability and safety can help lower feelings of shame and self-blame. It can also help people feel like they fit in and are accepted. Additionally, when families are involved in therapy, they can better understand the problems the child is having and give them the support and motivation they need to get better.

Families who have been touched by child sexual abuse can get help from a number of sources and services. Families can use these services to help them heal, build family ties, and improve their general health.

The Role of Cognitive Behavioral Therapy in Family Care

CBT is an important part of helping families who have been touched by child sexual abuse. Cognitive behavioral therapy (CBT) includes the whole family system, unlike other types of treatment that only work with one person. By understanding how family relationships are linked and how abuse affects each person, cognitive behavioral therapy (CBT) tries to improve family relationships and help people get better.

Family members are encouraged to be involved in therapy meetings so that they can talk about their worries and experiences and work together to get better. Therapists pay attention to the specific needs of each family member and give them the support and direction they need. Cognitive behavioral therapy (CBT) uses a joint method that makes sure everyone in the family feels heard, accepted, and able to help with the healing process.

One thing that might happen in a CBT session is that the therapist might lead a family conversation where everyone can talk about how the abuse has affected their lives. The therapist can then help the family come up with ways to help each other and get better.

The Impact of Family Care on the Healing Process

A child who has been sexually abused can heal a lot faster with the help and care of their family. Families who love, understand, and support their children no matter what lay the groundwork for their healing. A child can become more resilient, improve their mental health, and gain the strength to deal with the problems that come with being abused if they live in a home that supports them.

Testimonials and stories from families who have been through the mending process can show how family care can help. For instance, a family might talk about how therapy helped them trust each other again, talk to each other better, and make their relationships stronger. These people might talk about how learning more about the effects of abuse helped them give the child the support and direction they needed. These stories show how important family care and support can be in the rebuilding process.

Also, studies have shown that having a supportive family setting has effects that last longer than just helping someone get better. A study found that children who had been sexually abused and had families who were there for them were more likely to become resilient and have better long-term results than children who didn't have families who were there for them. This stresses how important care and support from family members are for a child's general health.

In the end, when there is child sexual abuse, it is very important to take care of the family. Cognitive behavioral therapy (CBT) is a complete and scientifically proven way to deal with the mental effects of abuse. CBT tries to heal families, build family bonds, and give people the tools they need to deal with the problems that come with abuse by focusing on the well-being of the whole family. CBT is very important for making sure that healing can happen in a safe and caring setting by teaching coping skills, giving information, and having the support of the parent or main caretaker who is not involved in the abuse.

Journey to Healing:

Don't be afraid to contact counseling services or someone you know if you or they need help or therapy because of child sexual abuse. Getting professional help is a big part of getting better, and there are tools out there to help families on their way.

Call to Action

If you are in need of immediate support or information related to child sexual abuse, consider reaching out to the following helplines and organizations:

- National Sexual Assault Hotline https://www.rainn.org/ 1-800-656-HOPE (4673)
- Childhelp National Child Abuse Hotline https://www.childhelp.org/ 1-800-4-A-CHILD (1-800-422-4453)
- Darkness to Light https://www.d2l.org/ A non-profit organization committed to ending child sexual abuse
- Military OneSource https://www.militaryonesource.mil/ A 24/7 gateway to information, resources, and support for military personnel and their families

These resources provide valuable information, support, and guidance for individuals and families affected by child sexual abuse. Remember, you are not alone, and there is help available to support you on your healing journey.

RESOURCES

- American Psychological Association (apa.org): Provides information on CBT and its applications in dealing with trauma, including child sexual abuse.
- National Child Traumatic Stress Network (nctsn.org): Offers resources on evidence-based treatments, including CBT, for children and families affected by trauma.
- Cognitive Behavioral Therapy for Children with Sexual Behavior Problems: A Retrospective Study - Journal of Child Sexual Abuse (tandfonline.com): An academic article discussing the application of CBT for children with sexual behavior problems offering insights for professionals and parents.
- Cognitive Behavioral Therapy for Children and Adolescents Experiencing PTSD: A Review of Meta-Analytic Findings - Psychiatry Journal (hindawi.com): A review of meta-analytic findings on the effectiveness of CBT for children and adolescents with PTSD, which can be relevant in cases of child sexual abuse.
- CBT for Children and Adolescents with High-Functioning Autism Spectrum Disorders by Angela Scarpa, Susan Williams White, and Tony Attwood: While not directly focused on child sexual abuse, this book explores CBT strategies for children and may offer insights into adapting CBT for specific needs.
- Cognitive-Behavioral Therapy for Children and Adolescents by Eva Szigethy and Christianne Esposito-Smythers: Provides practical guidance on applying CBT techniques to address various mental health challenges in children and adolescents.
- Journal of Child Sexual Abuse (tandfonline.com/journals): A journal that often publishes research articles on therapeutic interventions, including CBT, for children who have experienced sexual abuse.
- Association for Behavioral and Cognitive Therapies (abct.org): Offers information on finding CBT therapists, including those specializing in working with children who have experienced trauma.
- CBT for Child Trauma and Abuse (cbtforchilds.com): A website dedicated to providing information and resources on using CBT for children who have experienced trauma and abuse.

Journey to Healing:

| 11 |

Promoting Resilience and Recovery:
Empowering Survivors of Child Sexual Abuse

Sexual abuse as a child is a very stressful event that can have long-lasting effects on the mental and emotional health of those who have been through it. People who were sexually abused as children can have different effects, but in most cases, they have a lot of problems as adults, such as trust issues, low self-esteem, and mental health issues. But people who are resilient can have good things happen to them, like better mental health, higher self-worth, and a lower chance of being a victim again.

A range of studies has shown that between 10% and 53% of patients are able to work normally. To give survivors the best support and tools, it is important to know the long-term effects of child sexual abuse and come up with ways to help them stay strong and heal.

https://pubmed.ncbi.nlm.nih.gov/25389279
https://www.researchgate.net/publication/268232044%5FResilience%5Fin%5FSurvivors%5Fof%5FChild%5FSexual%5FAbuse

Understanding the Long-Term Effects of Child Sexual Abuse

To fully understand the long-term effects of child sexual abuse, it's important to know that they can look different for each victim. Some people may have responses and signs right away, while others may have delayed effects that show up later in life. Sexual abuse as a child can have a lot of different effects on a person's life, including their relationships, how they see themselves, and their general health.

For instance, sufferers of abuse may have trouble trusting others, which makes it hard for them to form close relationships. They might have shame, grief, and low self-worth, and they might blame themselves for the abuse they went through. Also, survivors may show signs of worry, sadness, and post-traumatic stress disorder (PTSD). These long-term effects can have a big effect on a survivor's quality of life, so it's important to give them the help and tools they need to be strong and heal.

Researchers have found that people who have been sexually abused as children can have a lot of different signs and problems that last into adulthood. Some of these are having trouble controlling your emotions, low self-esteem, and trouble making and keeping good connections. Child sexual abuse can also have physical effects. Survivors often have ongoing pain, stomach problems, and other health problems because of the stress they went through.

Strategies for Promoting Resilience in Survivors

Boosting the strength of people who have been sexually abused as children is very important for their healing and recovery. Being resilient means being able to get back on your feet after a setback and do well when things get tough. Many things can help it grow, such as social support, handling skills, and personal traits.

Support from family, friends, and experts is very important for helping people become strong. By making a space that is caring and helpful, you can help people feel understood and accepted, which can make them stronger. For instance, survivors who have a strong network of family and friends who believe and confirm what they've been through are more likely to be more resilient. These people can talk about their thoughts and feelings in a safe place, and they get help and guidance as they heal.

Coping techniques are also very important for helping people who have been sexually abused as children become more resilient. Survivors can better handle their feelings and deal with the problems they may face by learning healthy and useful ways to cope. Survivors can also speed up the healing process by doing things like going to therapy, taking care of themselves, and making new friends.

For example, people who go to therapy can benefit from having a safe and helpful place to work through their trauma, explore their feelings, and learn healthy ways to deal with things. Therapy gives people the skills they need to handle their feelings, question harmful ideas they have about themselves, and take charge of their lives again. Survivors can better understand what happened to them, learn how to deal with their problems, and start to heal by going to therapy.

https://onlinelibrary.wiley.com/doi/abs/10.1002/car.2258

Self-care tasks are another important way to help people become more resilient. Taking care of one's physical, social, and mental health is an important part of self-care. Survivors can do things like exercise, practicing awareness, and doing hobbies that make them happy and calm down. Survivors can take care of their physical and mental health by doing these things, and they can also help them be kind to themselves and accept themselves.

Approaches to Supporting Recovery in Survivors

For people who have been sexually abused as children, the healing process is complicated and different for each person. Therapy and the therapeutic relationship are very important in this process because they give people a safe and helpful place to talk about their trauma, work through their experiences, and learn healthy ways to cope. Therapy helps people deal with their feelings, come up with ways to heal, and become stronger.

Support from family and friends is also very important for building strength and getting better. Loved ones can help people heal by understanding, showing care, and confirming what they are going through. Friends and family can help a survivor feel safe and healthy by providing a loving and nonjudgmental space.

The National Sexual Assault Online Hotline is another helpful resource that offers free services to survivors of sexual assault. These services include private support, tools for healing and recovery, and connections for long-term support. People who have been through abuse can call the number and talk to trained support specialists who can help them in a way that fits their needs. This support can be very helpful for a survivor's healing by giving them the tools and direction they need.

https://www.rainn.org/about-national-sexual-assault-online-hotline

It's important to remember that the healing process may last longer or take longer for different survivors. Some people may need long-term treatment and support, while others may be able to heal with a mix of therapy, self-care, and help from friends and family. It is important to treat each survivor's journey with compassion, kindness, and understanding and to give them the tools and help they need to get better.

Overcoming Barriers to Resilience and Recovery

Child sexual abuse survivors may face many problems that make it harder for them to bounce back and get better. Survivors may not get the help and support they need because they are afraid of being judged, stigmatized, or embarrassed. Making an environment that is helpful and doesn't judge survivors is very important if you want to help them get past these problems and get the help they need to heal.

Raising knowledge and teaching people about child sexual abuse and its effects is important for reducing stigma and making the world a better place to live. Society can be more understanding and compassionate toward survivors' needs by learning more about them. Educating people about child sexual abuse can help bust myths and false beliefs, build understanding and kindness, and push survivors to get the help they need.

Healing Through Art Therapy

Those who have been sexually abused as children can use art therapy to help them heal. Art therapy gives people a safe way to talk about their feelings, work through their pain, and learn more about their experiences without using words. Painting, drawing, or sculpting are all forms of art therapy that can help people find themselves and heal.

Survivors can get their feelings and experiences out in the open through art therapy. This helps them see things from a different angle and find value in their suffering. Artists can help people heal by letting go of the feelings that they have been holding in. Art therapy also gives people a sense of control over their healing process by giving them a safe way to express themselves that makes them feel strong.

Empowering Survivors: Advocacy and Education

Educating and speaking out for sufferers of child sexual abuse are important ways to give them power and make society care about their well-being. Campaigns that teach people about child sexual abuse and make people more aware of it can help lower its incidence and make sure that survivors get the help and resources they need.

Advocacy work can also focus on pushing for structural changes, like better laws and policies that protect survivors, more money for support services, and better training for people who work with survivors. Being an advocate for survivors' rights and needs can help make society more understanding, helpful, and aware of what survivors go through.

Another important thing that can be done to help survivors is to support groups and tools that work on lobbying and education. People can help fund programs and projects that aim to raise awareness, offer support, and encourage survivors of child sexual abuse to be strong and heal by giving to these groups.

Supporting Loved Ones of Survivors

Helping the loved ones of survivors is an important part of building a strong support system that can help them get better. When a loved one deals with the effects of child sexual abuse on their relationship with the survivor, they may go through their problems and feelings. Giving survivors' loved ones a listening ear, showing understanding, and encouraging them to get professional help can be very helpful.

Family and friends should put their health and well-being first during this process. Caring for a victim can be hard on the emotions, so loved ones need to get help for themselves. This could mean going to therapy, joining a support group for survivors' loved ones, or doing things for themselves that are good for their mental health.

For survivors of child sexual abuse to heal and gain power, it is important to help them become resilient and recover. We can make a difference in the lives of survivors by knowing the long-term effects, using methods for resilience, and giving them support. As a society, we need to be more understanding and caring, and we should put survivors' education, lobbying, and health first. By working together, we can make a place where people who have been sexually abused as children can heal, become stronger, and look forward to a better future.

RESOURCES

- Rape, Abuse & Incest National Network (RAINN) - Survivors (rainn.org): Offers resources and support for survivors of sexual abuse, including information on recovery and empowerment.
- Joyful Heart Foundation (joyfulheartfoundation.org): Focuses on healing and empowerment for survivors of sexual assault, providing resources and support for the journey to recovery.
- Empowering Survivors: A Strengths-Based Trauma-Informed Framework - National Sexual Violence Resource Center (NSVRC) (nsvrc.org): A guide emphasizing a strengths-based, trauma-informed approach to empower survivors on their path to recovery.
- Resilience in Survivors of Child Sexual Abuse: A Descriptive Study - Journal of Interpersonal Violence (journals.sagepub.com): An academic article exploring factors contributing to resilience in survivors of child sexual abuse.
- The Body Keeps the Score: Brain, Mind, and Body in the Healing of Trauma by Bessel van der Kolk: Discusses the impact of trauma on the body and mind, providing insights into the healing process for survivors.
- Beyond Surviving: The Final Stage in Recovery from Sexual Abuse by Rachel Grant: Explores the stages of recovery and empowerment for survivors of sexual abuse.
- MaleSurvivor (malesurvivor.org): Focuses on supporting male survivors of sexual abuse, offering resources and community for empowerment.
- 1in6 (1in6.org): Dedicated to supporting men who have experienced sexual abuse or assault, providing resources for recovery and resilience.
- Trauma-Focused Cognitive Behavioral Therapy (TF-CBT) - National Child Traumatic Stress Network (nctsn.org): Provides information on TF-CBT, an evidence-based therapy approach for children and adolescents who have experienced trauma, including sexual abuse.
- Mindfulness-Based Stress Reduction (MBSR) - Center for Mindfulness (umassmed.edu): While not specifically focused on sexual abuse, MBSR is a mindfulness-based approach that can support survivors in managing stress and promoting well-being.

| 12 |

Tips to Strengthen Your Family:
Supporting Sexually Abused Children and Building Strong Bonds

To make a safe and caring place for families, it's important to strengthen family bonds and help children who have been sexually mistreated. These days, with everything going so quickly, it's more important than ever to put family ties first and make sure everyone is healthy. This chapter will talk about different ways to make your family stronger, encourage open conversation, and give sexually abused children the help they need. By doing these things, you can make your family stronger and more peaceful.

Importance of Family Support
Family support is very important for helping children who have been sexually abused heal and get better. When children go through such stressful events, having a caring family setting can make a big difference in their emotional and mental health. Family support gives the child a sense of safety, trust, and security, all of which are important for their healing.

    Please visit https://www.ncbi.nlm.nih.gov/pmc/articles/PMC7194188

Let's look at the story of Sarah and her family as an example. The family of Sarah, a young girl who had been sexually abused, trusted her and helped her in any way they could. They told her she could talk about how she felt and made sure she could go to skilled treatment. This network of support helped Sarah get through the hard times she was going through and eventually helped her heal.

As a family member, you need to actively listen to the child, confirm their experiences, and reassure them that you love and believe in them. It is very important to make sure that children feel safe enough to talk about their feelings and thoughts. Also, getting professional help, like therapy or counseling, can help the child and the family understand and deal with the effects of sexual abuse. Families can make a big difference in the health and healing of sexually abused children by giving them support and reassurance.

Tips for Strengthening Family Bonds

Strong family bonds are important for making sure that everyone in the family has a safe and loved place to live. For these strong ties to form, there must be open conversation. Everyone in the family can better understand and connect with each other if they are encouraged to say what they are thinking and feeling. This kind of open conversation can be made easier by setting aside time for family talks or having regular family meetings.

Another good way to improve family ties is to spend valuable time together. Family events like trips, game nights, and sports that everyone enjoys help people get closer to each other. For instance, planning a family hike or making a meal together gives everyone a chance to share an experience, which makes memories last longer and builds stronger ties.

It's important to show love, gratitude, and support for everyone in the family. Simple acts of kindness, like complimenting someone or saying thank you, can make family ties stronger. Regularly showing love and support for each other should be a top priority. This makes everyone in the family feel liked and respected, which makes the family stronger. Making family practices and routines is another good way to bring people together and make them feel like they belong. Whether it's a yearly family trip, a movie night that happens once a week, or a special holiday tradition, these habits give everyone a sense of belonging and help make memories that will last a lifetime. Family traditions give everyone a sense of stability and safety, which makes family ties stronger.

Parenting Tips for Caring for Sexually Abused Children

Being a parent of a child who has been sexually abused takes understanding and kindness. For these children's health and safety, creating a safe and caring space is very important. It is very important to earn the child's trust by being consistent, honest, and respectful. Parents need to make sure their children feel safe enough to talk about their feelings and experiences. It is important to listen to the child and support what they are saying. This will help them feel like they are being heard and understood.

It is very important to help children who have been sexually mistreated with their mental health needs. These children might have a lot of different feelings, like fear, shame, anger, and confusion. It is very important to give them a safe place to talk about their thoughts without fear of being judged. Parents should be gentle and understanding, and when things get hard, they should offer comfort and encouragement. They can also speed up the mending process by going to professional treatment. Trauma and child abuse specialists can give the child the support and direction they need to deal with their feelings and get better.

Parents can deal with problems that may come up by learning about the effects of sexual abuse and how people usually react to it. Parents can better help their children and meet their needs if they know what's going on. Setting limits and helping the child find good ways to deal with problems is important. Professional help and support groups can be very helpful in giving advice and encouragement.

For example, the Rape, Abuse, and Incest National Network (RAINN) gives parents and other adults who care for sexually abused children tools and assistance. On their website, you can learn how to spot signs of abuse, what to do about them, and how to help the child heal. They also have a service that parents can call to get help and support right away. Parents of a sexually mistreated child can get information and help from these sources to better care for their child.

https://genius.com/The-foundations-build-me-up-buttercup-lyrics

Characteristics of Problematic Families in Response to Sexual Abuse

When people in the family are told about accusations of sexual abuse, they may react in bad ways. Families with problems often play down or reject the accusations. Some families might blame the child or not believe what they say. This reaction can make the child feel even worse and make it harder for them to heal. You can also stall action and keep the child from getting the help and safety they need by denying or downplaying the accusations.

For the child's general health and happiness, it is very important to recognize and deal with these troubling family reactions. Families need to understand how important it is to validate the child's experience and give them the help and support they need. Families can make a safe place for healing and recovery by recognizing the abuse and taking the right steps to stop it.

Smith et al. (2019), for example, found that children whose families ignored or played down sexual abuse had higher rates of emotional distress and mental health problems than children whose families recognized and talked about the abuse. Denying or downplaying accusations can make the child feel alone, ashamed, and betrayed. Because of this, families need to deal with these negative reactions and give the child the support and approval they need.

https://www.ahajournals.org/doi/10.1161/JAHA.118.009305

Overcoming Denial and Minimizing Allegations of Sexual Abuse

Stopping the child from denying or downplaying claims of sexual abuse is an important step in helping them heal. The first step in giving the right kind of help is to acknowledge these reactions. If you want to get past these problems, you should get professional help, like therapy or counseling. Therapists can help families understand how sexual abuse works and help them deal with the complicated feelings that come up when people deny or downplay accusations.

Giving families information and tools about how sexual abuse works can help them understand how important it is to validate the child's experience. When families learn more about the effects of sexual abuse on children, they can better understand how it affects their health. This knowledge can help families get over their rejection and give their children the help they need to heal.

For example, Johnson et al.'s (2018) study shows how important it is to teach families about the effects of sexual abuse and how important support is. Families can better understand the long-term effects of denying and downplaying accusations by learning more about them. This information can give families the strength to get past the problems and give their children the help they need to heal. This link will take you to a book called NBK482376 at the National Library of Medicine.

Making a safe and caring space is also important for getting past denial and minimizing accusations. Setting clear limits and rules helps make a place safe for children who have been sexually abused. Having rules can help families make it safe for children to talk about their feelings without worrying about being judged or blamed. Getting people to talk to each other openly and honestly can make the setting more helpful. To get past the avoidance hurdles, families can make an environment where the child feels safe talking about their feelings.

Creating a Safe and Nurturing Environment

You should set clear rules and limits to make sure everyone feels safe and cared for. Making the child feel safe and secure in this way helps keep them safe. There are both physical and emotional limits. Physical boundaries include things like personal space and privacy. Emotional boundaries include things like appreciating each other's thoughts and feelings.

Another important part of making a safe and caring space is encouraging open conversation. Everyone in the family feels heard and understood when they are encouraged to say what they think and feel. Family talks or check-ins on a regular basis give everyone a chance to share their ideas and experiences. Parents need to listen to their children, understand how they feel, and help them when they need it.

Giving children access to support groups or therapy can be very helpful for both the children and their families. During the mending process, these tools can help and give advice. Support groups give the child and their family a chance to meet other people who have been through similar things. This can help them feel understood and accepted.

For instance, groups like RAINN offer online support groups where survivors and their families can meet other people who have been through the same things. These support groups give people a safe place to talk about their feelings, experiences, and ways of dealing with problems.

Resources for Parenting Tips and Family Support
Books, blogs, and support groups are all good places to get parenting advice and help for the whole family. These tools can help families who are having trouble by giving them advice and encouragement.

Aside from therapy, many books and websites offer advice on how to be a good parent and offer support for families. A well-known book called "The Courage to Heal" by Ellen Bass and Laura Davis advises people who have been sexually abused and their families. It tells the victim and their loved ones how to get through the healing process in a useful way.

Families who are dealing with sexual abuse can also find help and tools on websites like RAINN. Parents who are helping a child who has been sexually abused can find useful information and advice in these places. Parents and guardians can also get help from professional therapy services. They can help parents deal with the many feelings and problems that come up when they are taking care of a child who has been sexually abused. Therapists can help you set healthy limits, make your home a safe and caring place, and learn healthy ways to deal with stress. Overall, professional counseling services are very important for helping children and families who have been sexually abused heal and get better.

Supporting the Healing Process
Helping someone heal means making sure they have a safe and caring place to be, getting them to therapy, and giving them unwavering support. Children who have been sexually abused can get over their pain and become stronger through therapy. Children learn good ways to deal with their feelings and process them in treatment. Having the whole family in therapy meetings encourages open conversation and makes the family stronger.

Journey to Healing:

During the mending process, families need to offer support and encouragement all the time. Unconditional care is very important for the child's healing. Families should let the child know that they are loved, trusted, and supported. Parents must be gentle and understanding as their child goes through the process of healing.

According to Thompson et al. (2020), family assistance is very important for helping sexually abused children get better. The study discovered that children who got constant help from their families were emotionally healthier and more resilient than children who didn't get support. The study shows how important families are for helping children who have been sexually abused get better. Families can give a child the power to heal and become strong by always being there for them.

For children who have been sexually mistreated to be healthy and recover, family relationships must be strengthened, and they must receive assistance. Using the ideas and tips in this piece, families can make their home a safe and caring place that helps people heal and bounce back. Remember how important it is to report sexual abuse and get professional help so that the child can get the best help and protection.

RESOURCES

- Darkness to Light (d2l.org): Provides resources and tips for parents on preventing child sexual abuse and fostering a safe and supportive family environment.
- NSPCC - Support for Parents (nspcc.org.uk): Offers guidance and resources for parents on supporting children who have experienced sexual abuse, emphasizing building strong family bonds.
- Helping Your Child Heal After Sexual Abuse: What You Can Do - RAINN (rainn.org): A guide for parents on supporting their child's healing process after sexual abuse, including practical tips.
- Supporting Your Child After Sexual Abuse - Childhelp (childhelp.org): Provides information on how parents can support their child emotionally and create a nurturing environment.
- The Courage to Heal: A Guide for Women Survivors of Child Sexual Abuse by Ellen Bass and Laura Davis: While primarily for survivors, it also offers insights for families on supporting healing after child sexual abuse.
- Allies in Healing: When the Person You Love Was Sexually Abused as a Child by Laura Davis: Focuses on supporting partners and families of survivors, providing guidance on building understanding and empathy.
- Family Advocacy and Support Team - Darkness to Light (d2l.org): Offers information on building a family advocacy and support team to create a protective environment for children.
- Child Advocacy Centers (National Children's Alliance) - Find a Center (nca-online.org): Helps locate child advocacy centers that provide support services for families dealing with child abuse.
- Trauma-Focused Cognitive Behavioral Therapy (TF-CBT) - National Child Traumatic Stress Network (nctsn.org): Provides information on TF-CBT, a therapeutic approach for children and families dealing with trauma.
- Family-Based Therapy for Trauma (FBT-T) - The Trauma Center (traumacenter.org): Offers information on family-based therapy approaches for trauma, which can be beneficial for families dealing with the aftermath of child sexual abuse.

Journey to Healing:

| 13 |

Summarizing a Safe and Structured Home:
The Power of Rules and Boundaries

It is very important to set rules and limits in the home to keep everyone safe, provide order, and encourage good relationships between family members. Rule-based behavior helps children know what is expected of them and what the limits are. Rules are also very helpful for children who have been through a lot of bad things because they give them a sense of safety and consistency in their lives.

Making a unique family safety plan that takes into account each family member's wants and situations is another way to improve their safety and well-being. This will discuss why rules and limits are important in the home, how to make a specific family safety plan, and answer some common questions about family safety.

https://www.irs.gov/credits-deductions/energy-efficient-home-improvement-credit
https://www.hudexchange.info/programs/home/home-laws-and-regulations

The Benefits of Rules and Boundaries in the Home

Setting rules and limits at home is good for everyone. For starters, rules make things feel safe and predictable, which makes for a stable and caring atmosphere. It's better for children's mental health and less stressful for them when they know what's expected of them. As an example, a rule could say that children must do their chores before they can do anything fun. Setting this rule up helps children learn duty and discipline, and it also helps them stick to the pattern.

Second, rules help people be responsible and make good decisions. By making rules clear, parents help their children learn to be responsible for their actions and know what will happen if they make certain choices. Like, one rule could be that children need to clean up after themselves. Children learn how important it is to be responsible by following this rule. It also helps them form good habits that will help them throughout their lives.

In addition, rules and limits help family members talk to each other and get along well. It's easier for people to talk to each other and work together when everyone knows and follows the rules. Family members learn how to effectively communicate their wants and needs, which leads to better dispute settlement and stronger bonds. One rule could be that everyone in the family must turn around and speak at family meetings. It is important to follow this rule so that everyone can be heard. It also promotes respectful conversation and careful listening.

Self-discipline and respect can also be learned through rules. Children learn self-control and care for others' property and limits when they learn to follow the rules. This makes it easier to get along with others and understand their feelings. One rule could be that children should always ask their parents' permission before taking something from a sibling. This rule teaches children to respect other people's space and how important it is to ask for permission.

In the end, rules help people feel emotionally and mentally healthy. Making an organized and caring space for children makes them feel safe and important. This lets them explore their feelings, speak their minds openly, and build a good sense of who they are. Such a rule might say that family members should be kind and respectful to each other. This rule creates a safe space where everyone feels liked and valued.

Designing a Personalized Family Safety Plan
It is important to make a unique family safety plan that fits your family's wants and situations. Getting everyone in the family involved in the planning process is important to make sure that everyone owns the plan and sticks to it. Everyone having a say makes it more likely that everyone will work together and follow the safety plan. For instance, at a family meeting, parents can ask their children what they think about safety issues and possible answers.

First, think about the specific problems and wants your family may have. Think about things like your child's age, any health problems they may already have, and how your home is set up. This evaluation will help find possible dangers and places that need extra care. For example, if you have a baby, you might want to focus on making your home safe for children to avoid accidents.

Another step is to make sure the safety plan has clear goals and aims. Figure out what you want to happen, like lowering the number of crashes or supporting safety online. These goals will help us come up with plans and next steps. You should tell everyone in the family about these goals and make sure everyone knows what they need to do to reach them. To make fire safety better, for instance, family members can be given specific chores, like checking smoke alarms on a regular basis or making a fire escape plan.

An important part of a good family safety plan is including ways to encourage open conversation and trust. Encourage your family members to talk about their worries and ask questions on a regular basis. Creating a space where everyone feels safe talking about their fears and thoughts will help build trust and openness. For instance, you could set aside a certain time every week for a "safety check-in" where family members can talk about any worries they have about safety.

It is very important to review and update the family safety plan on a regular basis to make sure it works. If your family grows or your situation changes, you should make changes to the plan. Set up regular family meetings to talk about any changes or improvements to the plan and to address any new safety concerns that come up. This way of working together makes sure that everyone knows the plan and can help it succeed. For example, if your family is going to move to a new house, you should make it a priority to go over and update the safety plan to include any new risks or dangers that come with the move.

Addressing Safety in Specific Areas within the Home and Community

It's important to think about safety in certain parts of the home and neighborhood when making a family safety plan. First, make a list of possible dangers in different parts of the house, like the bedrooms, bathrooms, and outside areas. Some things that could be done are locking furniture, so it doesn't fall over, putting childproof locks on closets, and keeping cleaning supplies out of reach. One way to keep people from slipping and falling is to put down non-slip mats in the bathroom.

Adding safety features like smoke detectors, carbon monoxide monitors, and security systems can make your home much safer overall. These steps give early signs and protect against possible risks. For instance, putting in a security system can keep thieves away and give the whole family peace of mind.

Another important part of the family safety plan is teaching children how to stay safe in public places and online. Teach them how to stay safe around strangers, how to use public transportation safely, and how to spot and deal with online threats. You can make rules about how to use the internet, like not giving out personal information online and being careful when talking to people on social media.

It is very important to make emergency plans and processes for natural disasters and other unplanned events. Make sure everyone in the family knows what to do in case of a fire, an earthquake, or bad weather, and choose a place where everyone will meet. For instance, hold regular fire drills and talk about how to get out of the building and who to call in an emergency.

Working together with neighbors and neighborhood groups can make everyone safer by building a feeling of support and community. Get to know your friends and build ties with them that encourage helping each other and being careful. You could, for instance, start a neighborhood watch program or take part in safety-focused group projects.

Establishing and Reinforcing General House Rules

General house rules are very important for keeping your home safe and peaceful. Children can learn what is right and wrong by being told what is expected of them in terms of behavior and conduct. One rule that could be made is that everyone must clean up after themselves. This rule encourages people to be responsible and clean.

As examples of general house rules, people should always wear clothes, not wrestle, or tickle, and ask permission before using other people's things. These rules can be different for each family based on their morals and how they work together. For example, the rule that you should always wear clothes helps with personal cleanliness and gives you a sense of privacy in your own home. Also, it makes sure that everyone is safe and treated with care.

It's important to explain the reasoning behind each rule to help people understand and follow them. If children know why the rules are in place, they are more likely to follow them without complaining. For instance, when you talk about the rule that you need to ask permission before using someone else's things, you can stress how important it is to respect other people's property and how important agreement is.

For house rules to work, they need to be tailored to fit the family's ideals and way of life. When making rules for your family, think about how old each person is and what they need. For instance, rules for teens might be different from rules for little children. Making sure the rules are always followed and reinforced is important for making sure they work. For example, if someone breaks a rule repeatedly, there should be results to make them realize how important it is to follow the rule.

Tailoring the Safety Plan to the Unique Needs of the Family

When making a safety plan for your family, you should consider that every family is different and has different wants and situations. For the plan to work, it's important to understand and deal with these unique situations and problems. If a family member has a disability, for instance, the safety plan should include ways to make accommodations and meet their unique needs.

To make sure that everyone in the family is included and that the safety plan makes sense, it is important to get their feedback. By getting everyone involved, you can get useful ideas and views that can help the plan work better. If a family member knows a lot about technology, for example, their opinion can be helpful when talking about online safety issues.

It is important to make sure that the safety plan works for families with special needs, like those who have disabilities or who come from different cultures. Talk to professionals, like therapists or counselors, who can help you and your family in ways that are unique to their needs. These experts can give you good tips on how to deal with specific problems and make sure the safety plan is complete and useful.

It is also important to keep checking to see how well the safety plan is working. Check-in on a regular basis to see if the plan is working as planned and make any changes that are needed. The safety plan for your family should change as the needs of the family change. Be ready to listen to what people have to say and change the plan as needed to make sure it stays useful and current.

The Role of Boundaries in Protecting Sexually Abused Children
Setting clear limits is important for making a safe and loving space, especially for children who have been sexually mistreated. Setting limits gives children a sense of security and order, which helps them trust again and feel in charge again. For example, it's very important for their healing that you set limits on physical touch and personal space.

It is very important for the health of sexually mistreated children to know and set their limits. It is important to talk about personal limits and permission in an open way. Children should know it's okay to say "no" when they don't want to do something, and they should be able to say how comfortable they are. You can talk freely about body liberty and how important it is to respect personal limits, for example.

It's also important to give children the tools and support they need to understand and set limits. This could include therapy or coaching to help them work through their feelings and find good ways to deal with them. Working with professionals, like therapists or counselors, can help you come up with ways to set healthy limits and speed up the healing process. Therapists can help with things like making sure you know your limits and communicating clearly.

Effective Communication Strategies within the Family
A healthy and peaceful home atmosphere depends on people being able to talk to each other clearly. Stress how important it is for family members to talk to each other openly and honestly. Get family members to really listen to each other, which will help them understand and care about each other. Active hearing skills include things like keeping eye contact and recapping what the other person has said.

For the conversation to work, family members need to feel free to share their ideas and feelings. Set up a safe place where family members can talk about their worries and thoughts. For example, set aside a certain time every week for a "family check-in" where everyone can talk about their thoughts and feelings without holding back.

For family ties to stay healthy, disagreements must be solved through polite and helpful conversation. Teach your family members how to deal with disagreements by using "I" words and looking for areas where everyone can agree. For instance, tell family members they can talk about their problems and wants without yelling or calling each other names.

When family members get together on a regular basis, they can talk about problems, go over rules, and improve their ties. For example, you could have family meetings once a month to talk about any new safety issues, check in on how well the safety plan works, and stress how important it is to follow the rules. These meetings give people a chance to talk to each other and work together.

Seeking Professional Support for Family Safety
In some situations, getting professional help can make the family much safer and healthier. Getting pros like therapists or counselors involved

can help and give you tools. These experts can help deal with stress, boost conversation, and make family relationships stronger. For instance, therapy meetings can be a safe place for healing and growth for a family member who is having problems linked to trauma.

There are counseling services that can help you come up with good ways to keep your family safe. Therapists can give you the tools and skills you need to deal with specific problems and keep your family healthy. For example, they can help you come up with ways to deal with stress, communicate better, and settle disagreements.

Families can also get more help and tools from support groups or neighborhood groups. These groups give families a sense of community and understanding by putting them in touch with others who are going through the same things. For instance, there may be support groups just for families dealing with trauma or special safety issues.

When looking for professional help, it's important to pick people who are educated and have worked with families and children before. They can help you make a safe and caring workplace by sharing their knowledge and experience. Before choosing a therapist or counselor, for example, you can look into their qualifications and get suggestions from people you trust.

Setting rules and limits in the home and making a specific family safety plan is important for making sure that everyone is safe, healthy, and growing up properly. Rules give you order, encourage you to be responsible, and help your family get along well. A personalized family safety plan takes into account each family's unique wants and situations, making everyone safer and more secure.

Families can reduce the risks that might happen by focusing on safety in certain parts of the home and neighborhood. Making the safety plan fit the family's specific needs makes it more likely to work and be useful. Setting limits is an important part of keeping sexually abused children safe and helping them heal. Family communication techniques that work well help people understand, care about each other, and solve problems. Getting professional help can give you more advice and tools to make your family safer. Establishing rules, limits, and a personalized safety plan can help families make a safe and caring space where everyone can grow.

RESOURCES

- Child Welfare Information Gateway (childwelfare.gov): Offers resources and information on creating a safe and structured home environment, including guidelines on setting rules and boundaries.
- Positive Discipline (positivediscipline.com): Provides tools and articles on positive discipline strategies, emphasizing the importance of clear rules and boundaries in fostering a healthy family environment.
- "The Power of Structure: Creating a Home that Builds Resilience" - Psychology Today (psychologytoday.com): An article discussing the positive impact of structure and routines in creating a safe and nurturing home for children.
- "Setting Boundaries for Your Child" - American Academy of Pediatrics (healthychildren.org): A guide for parents on the importance of setting and communicating clear boundaries for children's well-being.
- Parenting from the Inside Out: How a Deeper Self-Understanding Can Help You Raise Children Who Thrive by Daniel J. Siegel and Mary Hartzell: Explores the connection between a parent's understanding of themselves and the creation of a secure and structured home environment.
- No-Drama Discipline: The Whole-Brain Way to Calm the Chaos and Nurture Your Child's Developing Mind by Daniel J. Siegel and Tina Payne Bryson: Focuses on discipline strategies that promote understanding and connection while maintaining clear boundaries.
- Parenting for Lifelong Health (plhprograms.org): Offers evidence-based parenting programs, including modules on setting rules and boundaries for a safe and structured home.
- National Institute of Child Health and Human Development (NICHD) - Parenting Resources (nichd.nih.gov): Provides resources on various aspects of parenting, including the establishment of rules and boundaries for child development.
- Circle of Security International (circleofsecurityinternational.com): Offers resources and programs for parents to enhance the parent-child relationship by understanding and meeting the child's emotional needs within secure boundaries.

Journey to Healing:

| 14 |

A Comprehensive Guide for Protecting and Parenting Sexually Abused Children:
Building Trust, Promoting Healing and Preventing Abuse

Sexual abuse of children is a terrible crime that affects many children's lives. It is very important for parents and other adults who care for children to know the signs and symptoms of child sexual abuse and how to make their home a safe and caring place for these children. In this detailed guide, we looked at many ways to protect and care for children who have been sexually abused, such as understanding child sexual abuse, making a safe space, fostering trust, getting professional help, giving children power, educating oneself, and helping parents and caregivers.

Understanding Child Sexual Abuse

Child sexual abuse is when a child is involved in sexual behaviors that they don't fully understand and can't agree to on their own. About one in four girls and one in thirteen boys have been sexually abused as children, so it is a widespread problem.

It is very important to know the signs and symptoms of child sexual abuse so that help can be given right away. Behavior changes, sudden fear or dislike of certain people, and accidents or pain that can't be explained are all common signs.

Go to https://www.rainn.org/about-national-sexual-assault-online-hotline to learn more.

For instance, a child who used to be friendly and sure of themselves might start to avoid people and show signs of worry or sadness. They may also act in ways that are backward, like wetting the bed or sucking their thumbs. Seeing these changes in behavior can be a sign that someone is being sexually abused.

Researchers have found that sexually abusing children can hurt their mental and physical health for a long time. It has been shown in studies that children who have been sexually abused are more likely to have anxiety, sadness, PTSD, and other mental illnesses. Offering these children, the support and tools they need to heal and get better is very important.

Creating a Safe and Supportive Environment

Making a safe and loving space is very important for the health and safety of children who have been sexually mistreated. To make sure they are physically and emotionally safe, you need to set clear limits and rules. Childproofing the house and keeping an eye on what children do online can also help stop more crimes from happening.

Along with these steps, it's important for family members to make open conversation and active listening a priority. By making it safe for children to talk about their worries and feelings, parents and other adults who care for them can better understand what they need and give it to them. Being honest with each other can also help the child and caretaker trust each other, which is very important for healing.

For instance, parents can start talking to their children about personal safety and setting limits. They can teach children about permission and help them understand that they can say "no" to any unwanted touch or approach. Parents can give their children the tools they need to protect themselves and get help if they need it by having these talks with them.

Building Trust and Promoting Healing
Children who have been sexually abused often have trouble believing others because they have been betrayed before. To build trust with a child, you need to be consistent, dependable, patient, and aware of their limits. To repair trust, it's important not to rush the process and to let the child set the pace.

Therapy is very important for getting better and restoring trust. Experts help children who have been sexually abused get better by using different types of therapy, such as cognitive-behavioral therapy and play therapy.

It's important to remember that trust takes time to build. It might take some time for a child who has been sexually mistreated to feel safe enough to talk to other people. Parents and caregivers can help the child heal and rebuild trust at their own pace by giving them a safe and loving space to live and getting professional help.

Seeking Professional Help and Support
For children who have been sexually abused to heal and get better, they need to get skilled help. People who have been sexually assaulted can get free, private help from groups like the National Sexual Assault Online Hotline. For survivors, it's a safe place to talk about what happened, get

help healing and getting better, and learn about the rules and tools in their community.

Parents and other caregivers should get skilled help, but they should also have their support crew. It can be hard for parents to support a child who has been sexually mistreated, so they should make time for self-care and get help when they need it.

Empowering Children and Teaching Personal Boundaries

Giving sexually mistreated children the tools, they need to take charge of their lives again is very important. A good way to teach children about personal limits and permission is through age-appropriate activities and talks. Parents can give their children the information and skills they need to stay safe by teaching them about safe touch and personal space.

Because of this, parents can teach their children that their bodies are theirs and no one else can touch them in a bad way. They can teach them how important it is to say "no" to any unwanted touch and to talk to an adult they trust if they feel dangerous or uncomfortable.

Parents can read suggested books with their children to help keep them from being sexually abused. These books talk about many things, like body liberty, setting personal limits, and what kinds of touches are safe and not safe. These are useful ways to start important talks about personal safety.

Educating Oneself about Child Sexual Abuse and Prevention

Parents and other caregivers should make it a priority to educate themselves on the prevention of child sexual abuse and abuse of children. Protecting children requires a number of important tasks, including gaining an understanding of the dynamics of child sexual abuse, detecting the warning signals, and learning how to prevent it from occurring.

Supporting the Healing Process
Helping children who have been sexually abused get better takes a wide range of actions. Therapy, like solo and group therapy, is a big part of helping children work through their problems and find ways to deal with them.

For example, group therapy can give children a safe place to talk about their problems and learn from others who have been through the same things. It helps them see that they're not the only ones going through this and that other people understand. Parents who go to group treatment can also meet other parents who are also caregivers, share their experiences, and get support from each other.

Preventing Child Sexual Abuse
Everyone needs to work together to stop sexual abuse of children. Parents can make a big difference by teaching their children about safety and setting limits. Children can protect themselves by having open, age-appropriate conversations about body control and what kinds of touches are acceptable and not appropriate.

Resources from groups like Parents Protect can help make people more aware of child sexual abuse and stop it. These links give you information on how to stay safe online, how to spot signs of abuse, and teaching tools that are right for your age. Parents can take precautions to keep their children safe by using these tools.

It's important to remember that attempts to stop violence should not just focus on one family. There are things that schools, neighborhood groups, and the government can do to stop sexual abuse of children. We can make a society that puts the safety and well-being of all children first if we all work together.

Giving Parents and Caretakers Help

It is important to help parents and other adults who care for children who have been sexually abused. It can be very hard on your emotions to help a child through the mending process. Parents and caregivers need to make time for self-care and get help when they need it.

Aside from professional help, it can be helpful to talk to other parents and caregivers who have been through the same things. Support groups or internet communities can help you feel understood, cared for, and accepted. It lets parents and guardians talk about the problems they're having, get help, and get support from people who understand what they're going through.

To sum up, protecting and parenting children who have been sexually abused takes a deep knowledge of the problem and effective ways to help. We can help these children heal and do well by making their surroundings safe and supportive, building confidence, getting professional help, giving children power, educating ourselves, and helping parents and other adults who care for them.

For everyone involved, stopping child sexual abuse is a job that needs to be done. Help make the world a better place for all children by staying informed, having open talks, and being there for each other. Let's work together to protect and care for the health and safety of sexually abused children and give them the chance to heal, grow, and do well.

I hope that a day will come that a book like this will not be needed, but until that happens, I hope the words on the previous pages will help you address the difficulties of child sexual abuse.

Until Then Take Care and Know that YOU Matter!

Rick

RESOURCES

- Darkness to Light (d2l.org): Provides resources on preventing child sexual abuse and offers guidance for parents on protecting and supporting sexually abused children.
- National Center for Missing & Exploited Children (missingchilds.org): Offers resources and guides for parents on preventing child sexual exploitation and providing support to abused children.
- Helping Your Child Heal After Sexual Abuse: What You Can Do - RAINN (rainn.org): A guide for parents on supporting their child's healing process after sexual abuse, including practical tips.
- Child Sexual Abuse: What Parents Need to Know - Child Welfare Information Gateway (childwelfare.gov): An informative guide for parents covering various aspects of child sexual abuse, including prevention and intervention.
- The Sexual Healing Journey: A Guide for Survivors of Sexual Abuse by Wendy Maltz: Offers insights for survivors and their families, providing guidance on healing after sexual abuse.
- The Body Keeps the Score: Brain, Mind, and Body in the Healing of Trauma by Bessel van der Kolk: Explores the impact of trauma, including sexual abuse, on the body and mind, offering insights for parents.
- Trauma-Focused Cognitive Behavioral Therapy (TF-CBT) - National Child Traumatic Stress Network (nctsn.org): Provides information on TF-CBT, an evidence-based therapy approach for children who have experienced trauma, including sexual abuse.
- Circle of Security International (circleofsecurityinternational.com): Offers resources and programs for parents to enhance the parent-child relationship, especially relevant for children who have experienced trauma.
- Stewards of Children - Darkness to Light (d2l.org): An evidence-informed training program for adults, including parents, on preventing child sexual abuse and providing support.
- Childhelp - Legal Information (childhelp.org): Provides legal information and resources for parents dealing with child sexual abuse cases, including reporting procedures.

Appendix A

Reacting to Sexual Abuse of Children
Exploring the Nature of Sexual Abuse

Any sexual contact between a minor and an adult without the minor's permission is considered sexual abuse. Everything from physical touch to exposure to sexually explicit content or conduct falls under this category. Keep in mind that children might not always be very forthright when explaining what they've been through. They may exhibit alterations in conduct, feelings, or bodily manifestations.

Indicators of Sexual Violence

- **Mood Shifts:** Unexpected shifts in mood or demeanor, including being more withdrawn, hostile, or secretive than normal.
- **Signs and symptoms:** Injuries, discomfort, or irritation in the genital area that do not have a clear cause.
- **Problems with Emotions:** PTSD symptoms, sadness, or anxiety.
- Bedwetting and thumb-sucking are examples of regressive behaviors. Unsuitable for a youngster of that age in terms of sexual knowledge or conduct.

Quick Actions Following Disclosure

- **Trust the Young One:** Praise their bravery in raising their voices. Tell me, "I believe you, and it's not your fault."
- **Remain Cool:** How you respond affects how comfortable they are sharing. Refrain from reacting angrily, horrified, or incredulously to the offender.
- **Consult a Doctor:** Make sure the child is physically healthy. Their well-being and legal proceedings may depend on the results of a medical test.
- **Make a Complaint:** Child protective services or local authorities should be contacted. For the child's protection and since it's the law, it's essential.

If the abuse has recently happened, do not bathe or change the child's clothes in order to preserve evidence.

Offering Sympathetic Assistance
- **Make Your Space Risk-Free:** They are safe in your house, and the abuse did not happen because of that.
- **Motivate Imagination:** When they are ready, let them express how they feel. Take the time to listen carefully and patiently.
- **Keep Things as They Are:** Maintaining consistent patterns might help establish stability.
- **Guidance from a trained expert:** Think about child abuse therapy. It is useful for mending mental and emotional scars.

Making Sense of the Legal System
- **Know Your Legal Protections:** Gain a better understanding of your rights and the legal processes by consulting with a lawyer who specializes in child abuse cases.
- **Get Ready for the Legal Process:** Have patience; the judicial process might drag on for a long period. Take part and stay informed.
- Provide emotional support by going with the child to any interviews or court appearances.

Recovery and Healing Over the Long Run
- The child and their family must participate in ongoing therapy. It helps the body recover over time.
- **Gather Support:** Get in touch with organizations that help families who have been victims of sexual abuse. Communicating one's story can have a healing effect.
- Find out what it's like to be a victim of sexual assault, how to cope, and how to trust again by educating yourself.
- The best way to empower a child is to encourage them to follow their passions. This helps them regain self-assurance and a feeling of normalcy.

Future Child Safety Measures
- They need to learn about their body rights and how to set healthy limits in order to develop autonomy over their bodies.
- Encourage open dialogue by creating a space where children feel comfortable bringing up any subject.
- **Keep an Eye Out for Red Flags:** Adults who might be dangerous should have their warning signals observed. Listen to your gut.
- Promote awareness of the risks associated with using the internet. Keep tabs on online activity without prying into personal lives.

In summary

Even though it's not easy, survivors of sexual abuse may recover with the help of those who care about them. A feeling of normality and safety, along with trust, love, and support, may be restored on this journey with your child. Keep in mind that some communities and services are prepared to lend you a helping hand.

Messages of Hope for the Child

There is support for you, and you are courageous. You deserve to be secure and happy regardless of what happened to you. You are not alone; those who truly care about you will be there to lend you a hand. Keep in mind that it's normal to experience and express negative emotions like sadness, fear, and anger. There is hope for your recovery and future.

Parents dealing with the distressing issue of child sexual abuse can find a thorough overview in this booklet. With the family's and the child's health and rehabilitation as our top priorities, we aim to provide clear, practical measures and reassuring advice to help you through this difficult time.

Journey to Healing:

Appendix B

Here's a list of websites that offer support, information, and guidance for parents in such situations:

- **Darkness to Light (d2l.org):** Provides educational resources and support for parents on preventing and responding to child sexual abuse.
- **RAINN (rainn.org):** Offers a comprehensive guide for parents on understanding and responding to child sexual abuse, along with a helpline for support.
- **Stop It Now! (stopitnow.org):** Focuses on preventing child sexual abuse and provides resources for parents to protect their children.
- **National Children's Alliance (nca-online.org):** Offers information on child advocacy and resources for parents dealing with the aftermath of abuse.
- **Childhelp (childhelp.org):** Provides resources and support for parents dealing with child abuse, including information on prevention and intervention.
- **The National Center for Victims of Crime (victimsofcrime.org):** Offers a variety of resources for parents, including guides on talking to children about abuse and understanding the legal process.
- **NSPCC (nspcc.org.uk):** The UK-based National Society for the Prevention of Cruelty to Children offers resources and guidance for parents on child protection.
- **American Academy of Pediatrics (aap.org):** Provides articles and guidance on recognizing and preventing child sexual abuse, with a focus on health and well-being.
- **Prevent Child Abuse America (preventchildabuse.org):** Offers resources for parents aimed at preventing child abuse and promoting healthy parenting practices.
- **Safe Horizon (safehorizon.org):** Provides support for victims of abuse and their families, with resources for parents on understanding and responding to abuse.

Journey to Healing:

Appendix C

The following is borrowed from the FACTSHEET for FAMILIES (December 2018) from the Child Welfare Information Gateway.

Parenting a Child or Youth Who Has Been Sexually Abused: A Guide for Foster and Adoptive Parents

As a parent or caregiver of a child or youth who has a known or suspected history of being sexually abused, you may feel confused about the impact of the abuse and uncertain about how you can help. It may be comforting to know that most children and youth who have been abused do not go on to abuse others, and many live happy, healthy, successful lives. At the same time, all children and youth who have been abused need to feel safe and loved in nurturing homes. As a parent or caregiver, you can play a central role in your child's healing process, as well as in "building resilience," which strengthens your child's ability to adapt to or cope with adversity.

This factsheet discusses how you can help children and youth in your care by educating yourself about child sexual abuse, understanding the impact of the abuse, establishing guidelines for safety and privacy in your family, and seeking help if you need it. Reading this factsheet alone will not guarantee that you will know what to do in every circumstance, but you can use it as a resource for some of the potential challenges and rewards that lie ahead.

For more information, see Child Welfare Information Gateway's webpage, Identification of Sexual Abuse, at
https://www.childwelfare.gov/topics/can/identifying/ sex-abuse.

Journey to Healing:

Journey to Healing:

www.ingramcontent.com/pod-product-compliance
Lightning Source LLC
LaVergne TN
LVHW051125080426
835510LV00018B/2235

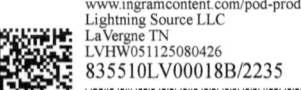